SHEPHERD'S NOTES

SHEPHERD'S NOTES

When you need a guide through the Scriptures

Genesis

BROADMAN
&HOLMAN
PUBLISHERS

Nashville, Tennessee

Shepherd's Notes, *Genesis*
© 1997 Broadman & Holman Publishers, Nashville, Tennessee
All rights reserved
Printed in the United States of America

ISBN# 0–8054–9028–0

Dewey Decimal Classification: 222.11
Subject Heading: BIBLE. O.T. GENESIS
Library of Congress Card Catalog Number: 97–28707

Library of Congress Cataloging-in-Publication Data
Genesis / Paul Wright, editor
   p. cm.—(Shepherd's notes)
   Includes bibliographical references.
   ISBN 0–8054–9028–0 (tp)
   1. Bible. O.T. Genesis—Study and teaching.
   I. Wright, Paul, 1955– . II. Series.
BS1239.G37 1998
222'.1107—DC21

97–28707
CIP

1 2 3 4 5 6   02 01 00 99 98 97

CONTENTS

FOREWORD

Dear Reader:

Shepherd's Notes are designed to give you a quick, step-by-step overview of every book of the Bible. They are not meant to be a substitute for the biblical text; rather, they are study guides intended to help you explore the wisdom of Scripture in personal or group study and to apply that wisdom successfully in your own life.

Shepherd's Notes guide you through both the main themes of each book of the Bible and illuminate fascinating details through appropriate commentary and reference notes. Historical and cultural background information brings the Bible into sharper focus.

Six different icons, used throughout the series, call your attention to historical-cultural information, Old Testament and New Testament references, word pictures, unit summaries, and personal application for everyday life.

Whether you are a novice or a veteran at Bible study, I believe you will find *Shepherd's Notes* a resource that will take you to a new level in your mining and applying the riches of Scripture.

In Him,

David R. Shepherd
Editor-in-Chief

Shepherd's Notes for Genesis is an easy-to-use tool for getting a quick handle on this significant Bible book's important features and for gaining an understanding of its message. Information available in more difficult-to-use reference works has been incorporated into the *Shepherd's Notes* format. This brings you the benefits of many more advanced and expensive works packed into one small volume.

The titles in the *Shepherd's Notes* series are for laymen, pastors, teachers, small-group leaders and participants, as well as the classroom student. Enrich your personal study or quiet time. Shorten your class or small-group preparation time as you gain valuable insights into the truths of God's Word that you can pass along to your students or group members.

DESIGNED FOR QUICK ACCESS

Bible students with time constraints will especially appreciate the time-saving features built into the *Shepherd's Notes*. All features help the student experience a quick and concise encounter with the heart of the message of Genesis.

Concise Commentary. The Book of Genesis is filled with characters, places, events, and instruction to believers. Short sections provide quick "snapshots" of the book's narratives and arguments, highlighting important points and other information.

Outlined Text. A comprehensive outline covers the entire text of Genesis. This is a valuable feature for following the narrative's flow, allowing for a quick, easy way to locate a particular passage.

Shepherd's Notes. These summary statements appear at the close of every key section of the narrative. While functioning in part as a quick summary, they also deliver the essence of the message presented in the sections that they cover.

Icons. Various icons in the margin highlight recurring themes in the book of Genesis, aiding in selective searching or tracing of those themes.

Sidebars and Charts. These specially selected features provide additional background information to your study or preparation. These include definitions as well as cultural, historical, and biblical insights.

Maps. These are placed at appropriate places in the book to aid your understanding and study of a text or passage.

Questions to Guide Your Study. These thought-provoking questions and discussion starters are designed to encourage interaction with the truth and principles of God's Word.

DESIGNED TO WORK FOR YOU

Personal Study. Using the *Shepherd's Notes* with a passage of Scripture can enlighten your study and take it to a new level. At your finger tips is information that would require searching several volumes to find. In addition, many points of application occur throughout the volume, contributing to your personal growth.

Teaching. Outlines frame the text of Genesis, providing a logical presentation of the message. Capsule thoughts designated "Shepherd's Notes" provide summary statements for presenting the essence of key points and events. Application icons point out personal application of the message of the book. Historical Context and Cultural Context icons indicate where background information is supplied.

Group Study. *Shepherd's Notes* can be an excellent companion volume to use for gaining a quick but accurate understanding of the message of Genesis. Each group member can benefit by having his or her own copy. The *Note's* format accommodates the study of themes throughout Genesis. Leaders may use its flexible features to prepare for group sessions or use them during group sessions. Guiding Questions can spark discussion of the key points and truths of the message of Genesis.

LIST OF MARGIN ICONS USED IN GENESIS

 Shepherd's Notes. Placed at the end of each section, a capsule statement that provides the reader with the essence of the message of that section.

 Old Testament Reference. Used when the writer refers to Old Testament Scripture passages that are related or have a bearing on the passage's understanding or interpretation.

 New Testament Reference. Used when the writer refers to New Testament passages that are related to or have a bearing on the passage's understanding or interpretation.

 Historical Background. To indicate historical, cultural, geographical, or biographical information that sheds light on the understanding or interpretation of a passage.

 Personal Application. Used when the text provides a personal or universal application of truth.

 Word Picture. Indicates that the meaning of a specific word or phrase is illustrated so as to shed light on it.

Genesis is a book of beginnings—the origin of the world, human history, families, sin, and the plan of redemption. The story line of Genesis ranges from the vastness of the universe to the intimacy of close family relationships.

The title of the first book of the Bible, Genesis, means "beginnings." The name of the book in Hebrew—the language in which it was first written—is "in the beginning," the book's opening phrase.

The book's first eleven chapters confront life's ultimate issues: the existence of God, the problem of evil, the meaning of life and humanity's place in an awesome universe. Chapters 12–50 focus on the attempt of four generations of the family of Abraham—ancestors of peoples of the Middle East but spiritual parents of us all (Gal. 3:6–9)—to live rightly in a difficult world. Through it all, Genesis boldly and unapologetically declares that God is involved in every detail of human life.

AUTHOR AND DATE OF WRITING

The Book of Genesis gives no indication as to its author. The title of the book in some English translations, "The First Book of Moses Called Genesis," is not part of the inspired text but reflects an early Christian and Jewish tradition. According to this tradition, Moses wrote the five books of the Pentateuch (Genesis, Exodus, Leviticus, Numbers, and Deuteronomy) during the time that Israel wandered in the wilderness. Jesus apparently accepted the Mosaic authorship of the Pentateuch because He called the first five books of the Bible "the Law of Moses" (Luke 24:44).

While it is proper to speak of Moses as the author of the Pentateuch, there is evidence within the Bible that he was guided by the Holy Spirit to use existing written or oral sources for

The issue of the authorship of Genesis is important because it is closely related to matters concerning the book's historical context, purpose, and meaning. However, questions about the authorship and date of Genesis must not be allowed to overshadow our response to its clear teachings. In the words of Thomas Á Kempis: "Search not who spoke this or that, but mark what is spoken."

—Thomas Á Kempis, *Of the Imitation of Christ,* v. 1

some of his information (see Num. 21:14, for example). In this way, Moses' writing activity was similar to that of Luke (Luke 1:1–4). Other verses in the Pentateuch suggest a minimal amount of editorial "updating" after the death of Moses (see Deut. 34:10–12; Gen. 14:14; cp. Judg. 18:29), but Moses was clearly responsible for the core of the Pentateuch.

Except for Jesus, no character in biblical history towers higher than Moses. The identity of ancient Israel and hence the core of Scripture is founded on two great events mediated by him—the Exodus from Egypt and the giving of the Law on Mt. Sinai. Whether working as a shepherd for his father-in-law or interceding on behalf of the Israelite masses, Moses' life was lived in the service of God and his people. Moses was Israel's deliverer, lawgiver, prophet, judge, author, and spiritual father.

Moses lived in either the fifteenth or the thirteenth century B.C. The life of Moses is dated by evidence that first dates the Exodus from Egypt and the conquest of Canaan by Joshua. This evidence, which includes literary, historical, archaeological and social scientific data, is complex and largely inconclusive. Because scholars are divided in their interpretation of the evidence, it is difficult to state an exact date for the composition of the Pentateuch.

AUDIENCE

The five books of the Pentateuch, all written by Moses and tied together in structure and theme, were originally intended to be read as a single work by a specific audience. That audience was the generation of Israelites who were ready to enter the Promised Land under Joshua's leadership. This territory had been promised to Abraham about four hundred years earlier.

This was to be *their* Promised Land, given by God Himself so that His chosen people, Israel, might live full and blessed lives and draw others to Him. But Canaan was a strange land to the Israelites, presenting numerous challenges to their physical, social, and spiritual well being.

PURPOSE

With such significant change at hand, Israel needed both reassurance and direction about many questions. Who is God? Who am I? Where can I find security and meaning in life? Have things *really* changed, or does life go on much as it always has?

Moses sought to prepare his people by providing for them a history and a future—both roots and shoots. The first portion of the Pentateuch, Genesis, offered the Israelites a past rooted in the very land that they were about to enter. Most of the rest of the Pentateuch supplied detailed instructions for living successfully once they entered this land. By obeying God, the Israelites could branch out into communities of blessing and peace.

God, the divine author of the Pentateuch, guided Moses so that his words would speak with equal relevance to audiences of all generations. Readers of Genesis throughout the ages have found answers to the ultimate questions of life.

STRUCTURE AND CONTENT

Genesis divides naturally into two major sections. Chapters 1–11, called the primeval history, covers four great events that affected the entire world: Creation, the Fall, the Flood, and the confusion of languages at Babel. Chapters

And God said to Abram, "Know for certain that your descendents will be strangers in a land that is not theirs, where they will be enslaved and oppressed four hundred years. But I will also judge the nation whom they will serve; and afterward they will come out with many possessions" (Gen. 15:13–14, NASB).

"Indeed, ask now concerning the former days which were before you, since the day that God created man on the earth, and inquire from one end of the heavens to the other. Has anything been done like this great thing, or has anything been heard like it?
Has any people heard the voice of God speaking from the midst of the fire, as you have heard it, and survived? Or has a god tried to go to take for himself a nation from within another nation by trials, by signs and wonders and by war and by a mighty hand and by an outstretched arm and by great terrors, as the LORD your God did for you in Egypt before your eyes? (Deut. 4:32–34, NASB).

12–50, the patriarchal history, recounts the lives of four great men called by God to be the ancestors of His special people: Abraham, Isaac, Jacob, and Joseph. Genesis thus begins with God and the world and ends with God and a family. The relationship between these three— God, the world, and those who belong to His family—is a dominant theme throughout the rest of the Bible.

LITERARY STYLE

Genesis is broadly classified as historical narrative. The stories of Genesis are of varying character and length. The story of Joseph, for example (chaps. 37–50), has features of a modern short story. On the other hand, the story of Cain and Abel (chap. 4) is closer to a vignette. Many of the stories of Genesis are tied together by genealogical material, some of which includes storylike features (see 4:20–22; 5:29).

Genesis is also historical. The stories of Genesis are a straightforward, plain (although artistic) telling of what happened in the past. Genesis gives every indication that its author, Moses, intended to write history and that he meant for his book to be read realistically.

The Book of Genesis displays great literary artistry. Moses skillfully wove a variety of literary forms into a single, beautifully variegated tapestry called Genesis. These include wordplay, metaphor, simile, pun, irony, allusion, paradox, and the patterned repetition of words, phrases, themes, or ideas. Moses' masterful use of language helps to make Genesis a fascinating book to read and draws us as readers into his story.

THEOLOGY

The Pentateuch, or Torah, is the first of three divisions of the Hebrew canon (Torah, the

Prophets, and the Writings), books which believers call the Old Testament.

The Pentateuch focuses on the grand theme of restoration. *All of God's creation, and especially people, have been adversely affected by sin and stand in need of restoration.* God chose to reconcile Himself to His errant creation by restoring people to a position in which they could have a relationship with Him. Each book of the Pentateuch contributes necessary theological elements to the development of this theme:

While the word *Torah* is usually translated "law," it more properly means "instruction." By giving His own special people the Torah (Exod. 19:3–6), God sought to prepare them to live meaningful lives in Canaan, their Promised Land. For this reason, God guided Moses to write the Pentateuch in such a way that its stories would emphasize the triad of God, people, and land.

BOOK	THEMATIC FOCUS
Genesis 1–11	Beginnings
Genesis 12–50	Promise
Exodus	Redemption
Leviticus	Holiness
Numbers	Testing
Deuteronomy	Instruction

Genesis sets the theological stage for the Pentateuch. Genesis 1–11, the primeval history, is a story of beginnings set on a universal scale. In these chapters, God is presented as a Creator who is totally in charge of His creation.

People, uniquely made in His image, are intended to be the crown of creation and have dominion over it. God's desire is to have a relationship with all people; Moses uses the image of "walking with God" throughout the Pentateuch to express this relationship. Because of man's willful disobedience, this potential for a relationship with God has become broken. God responds to people with either judgment or grace, requiring that everyone believe in Him.

The theme of chapters 12–50, the patriarchal history, is promise. God promised Abraham that his descendants would one day become a great nation and live in the land of Canaan. He also promised that the world would be blessed through them (12:1–3; 13:15–16; 15:4–5, 12–21; 17:3–8, 19–20; 18:18; 22:15–18). This promise was ratified through a covenant that God made with Abraham.

God's promise was restated to Abraham's son Isaac (26:3–4) and his grandson Jacob (28:13–15; 35:11–12; 46:2–4). These patriarchs had faith in God and believed in Him, even though the promise remained largely unfulfilled during their lifetimes (15:6; 50:24; cp. Heb. 11:8–22).

THE MEANING OF GENESIS FOR TODAY
The events described in Genesis took place thousands of years ago in a land halfway around the world. Moses' description of these events was written to meet specific needs of his contemporaries. Yet, the Book of Genesis is relevant even today.

For since by a man came death, by a man also came the resurrection of the dead. For as in Adam all die, so also in Christ all shall be made alive (1 Cor. 15:21–22, NASB).

For Christians, Genesis holds meaning because it anticipates the work of Jesus Christ. Genesis speaks of the Messiah. The promise of descendants made to Abraham ultimately finds its fulfillment in Jesus (12:2; 49:10), the "seed" of Adam who would destroy Satan and the power of sin (3:15). Jesus was the "last Adam" who overcame the effects of sin committed by the first Adam (Rom. 5:12–21).

Genesis is also relevant for Christians because many of the persons or events described in the book are pictures (or "types") of the Church. The true descendants of Abraham are all those, Jew and Gentile, who in faith accept the work of

Christ (Rom. 4:11–12, 16–25; Gal. 3:6–9, 29). When Jesus said that He had come so those who believe in Him "might have life and might have it abundantly" (John 10:10, NASB), He spoke of a life in which the promises of blessing had been fulfilled.

Because it speaks of beginnings, Genesis also has a built-in eschatalogical (or "end times") character. The promise of a land made to Abraham is detected in the heavenly Jerusalem (Heb. 11:8–10). The destruction and re-creation of the world found in Gen. 6–9 anticipates the new heaven and new earth written about by Isaiah (Isa. 65:17–25) and John (Rev. 21:1–22:5).

Genesis also appeals to the needs and desires of all people. The stories of Genesis confront issues of life, death, evil, meaning, and existence. Like Adam, all people sin (Rom. 5:12). Like Abraham, all humans long for security. Like Isaac, all of us fall victim to the actions of others. Like Jacob, all strive for advantage. Like Joseph, all face personal setbacks. Some people, like Abel, are cut down in their prime. Others, like Rebekah, are industrious and successful. Like us, most humans are enigmatic. Like us, all need God.

CREATION (1:1–2:25)

The Bible begins with God. It does not explain God's existence, nor does it start with God and then set Him aside. Rather, the Bible opens deliberately and quite unapologetically with the simple yet unfathomable words, "In the beginning God created . . . ," then relates how God is intimately involved in every aspect of creation.

The First Creation Account (1:1–2:3)

The opening two chapters of Genesis actually include two complementary stories of Creation. The first, Gen. 1:1–2:3, is a systematic account

Moses began the Pentateuch with the Creation, not simply because the origin of the universe was the first thing that happened in space-time reality, but because he understood that knowledge of our origins is crucial for understanding ourselves.

The Hebrew word translated by the English verb "to create" occurs in the Bible with only God as its subject. That is, while people can make things, only God creates. The basic idea of "create" is that of initiating something brand new, out of nothing. The phrase "God created" is used in three places in Gen. 1: For the creation of the heavens and earth (1:1), for the creation of the first living beings (1:21), and for the creation of people (1:27).

The word was also a favorite of the prophet Isaiah, who used it eighteen times, including once to refer to salvation (Isa. 45:8)—another thing that only God can do.

of the creation of the world. The second, Gen. 2:4–25, focuses on the creation of people and their responsibilities in the Garden of Eden.

In the beginning (1:1–2)

The first two verses of Genesis form an introduction to the creation story.

The statement of Gen. 1:1 is absolute and complete: "In the beginning God created the heavens and the earth." Everything was created by God out of nothing—*creatio ex nihilo*. This verse immediately takes the reader of Genesis into the vastness of time and space. The opening phrase marks the absolute beginning of time and the closing words refer to the entire universe.

In spite of the vastness of the created space-time universe, Moses described Creation on a scale that could be grasped by his audience. The words *heaven* and *earth* can also be translated "sky" and "land," thus turning the eyes of the reader toward the earth as a special place that God was preparing for people.

Genesis 1:2 describes an initial, preparatory stage of Creation. The earth as described in verse 2 was characterized by Moses in three ways: It was "without form and void," "darkness was upon the face of the deep," and "the Spirit of God moved upon the face of the waters." Together, these three statements indicate that the new earth was in a pristine state, not yet ready for human habitation.

The Hebrew words translated "without form and void" elsewhere describe an "empty" land or "wasteland" (Isa. 34:11; Jer. 4:23)—a land uninhabitable, like the wilderness through which Moses led the Israelites (Deut. 32:10). Moses evidently chose to describe the pristine earth as a desert to help wandering Israel understand that just as God had prepared the entire earth for human habitation, so He was also leading them out of a desert and into a specially prepared homeland.

The phrases *the face of the deep* and *the face of the waters* similarly describe a world unsuitable for human habitation. But rather than expressing the meaning of too little water as in a desert, this condition is one of too much water.

It would be improper from a scientific point of view to ask how the pristine earth could have been both a desert wasteland and a deep sea. The words used by Moses were highly descriptive, but not in the terms of modern scientific categories. While nothing in Genesis contradicts the facts of modern science when the limitations of science are properly understood, it must be remembered that Moses wrote with theological—rather than scientific—questions in mind.

Most attempts to correlate scientific data with Genesis have been tentative or inconclusive. Scientific theories change; scriptural truth does not.

Genesis 1:2 introduces an aspect of the character of God that becomes more fully developed as Scripture unfolds. Moses noted that the "Spirit of God" hovered over the face of the waters. Most Christians believe that the Spirit of God in Gen. 1:2 was the Holy Spirit. Like an eagle hovers over its young (Deut. 32:11), the Spirit of God hovered over and protected the yet-to-be-finished earth. According to Francis Schaeffer, "The universe had a personal beginning—a personal beginning on the high order of the

Why would God create the earth first to be uninhabitable? Doesn't it go against his character to make something that is not from the outset perfect and complete? Not necessarily. Christians, too, are "projects" on which God works. Although we are "new creations" in Christ (2 through deliberate acts of obedience and grace that we become "perfect and complete, lacking in nothing" (James 1:4, NASB; cp. Phil. 1:6). Similarly, it was only through successive acts of creation that the world became a perfect and complete place for people to live.

Deep waters are often used in the Pentateuch and other Old Testament books to portray a deadly threat to human existence (see Gen. 7:11; 8:2; Exod. 15:8; Pss. 69:1; 107:26; Amos 7:4; Jon. 2:5). Perhaps for this reason, the first characteristic of the new heavens and new earth noted by John was that the sea was "no more" (Rev. 21:1).

Later biblical writers understood well that the word of God encompassed a reality much greater than the spoken acts of Creation. God's revelatory words, spoken to Moses at Mt. Sinai, created a new people and instructed them in righteous living (Exod. 20:1; 34:28; Ps. 119:9). God's words empowered His prophets to minister as divine spokesmen (Isa. 1:2; 6:6–10). God's words are "firm in the heavens" (Ps. 119:89) and will "stand forever" (Isa. 40:8). John's insights are most profound: "In the beginning was the Word," Jesus Christ, the incarnate revelation of God, and "through him all things were made" (John 1:1–3).

Trinity" (*Genesis in Space and Time*, [InterVarsity Press, 1972], 21).

- *God made everything out of nothing. The*
- *first stage of Creation was a world that was*
- *not yet suitable for human life. Because God*
- *began the world this way, we can be sure that*
- *He will also prepare us, His "new creations,"*
- *to live lives suitable for His work and glory.*

The Six Creative Days (1:3–31)

Each of the six creative days is described from a terrestrial viewpoint, as if someone were standing on the earth watching God at work. While there obviously were no human witnesses to the Creation, Moses felt it important to involve his audience as literary spectators. In this way, the intimacy between God and His creation cannot be missed.

Moses' description of the six creative days is patterned, as the following chart indicates. With few exceptions, each phrase—sometimes with slight variation—is repeated for each day.

CREATION PHRASE	DAY 1	DAY 2	DAY 3	DAY 4	DAY 5	DAY 6
"God said, 'Let there be'"	1:3	1:6	1:9	1:14	1:20	1:24
"And it was so"	1:3	1:7	1:9	1:15	----	1:24
"God saw that it was good"	1:4	---	1:12	1:18	1:21	1:25
"God called"	1:5	1:8	1:10	----	----	----
"There was evening and there was morning, ___ day"	1:5	1:8	1:13	1:19	1:23	1:31

This formulaic patterning gives a poetic quality to the chapter, pointing to the orderliness and care by which God created. Each phrase reveals something about God and His plan for the world.

God began each creative act with the deliberate and decisive statement, "Let there be." God created effortlessly, with but a word. Each element of creation was an expression of Himself, spoken from deep within His being (cp. Heb. 11:3).

God spoke "and it was so." From the beginning of time, nothing was too hard for God or was kept from happening if He so willed (cp. 50:20).

After each creative day except one, God saw that what He had done was "good." The goodness of creation can be understood in at least two ways. First, because God is good (Ps. 25:8; Mark 10:18) His creation must reflect the goodness of His character. Second, the goodness of creation suggests that everything necessary for proper human life was in place. After people were created, God saw that everything was "very good" (1:31).

God "called," giving names to the elements created on the first three days. Granting someone or something a name in ancient times implied ownership and hence control. By naming things such as light, darkness, sky, water, and dry land, God declared His ownership over the forces of nature and power over the fertility gods thought to control nature.

The account of each creative day ends with the phrase, "And there was evening and there was morning, __ day." Moses intended for his readers to understand creation in terms of the days of a week (cp. Exod. 20:8–11; 31:17). For the Jews the twenty-four-hour period called "day" begins in the evening, at sundown. Whether Moses' description corresponds to six actual

Much has been made of parallels between the creation account of Gen. 1 and various creation stories from the ancient Near East. The best known is the Babylonian creation story Enuma Elish, "When on High." This story represented the prevailing creation theology of the day. In this account, the various elements of the cosmos (water, land, the heavenly bodies) were formed as the result of the procreation of the gods and goddesses. People were made only as an afterthought to serve the gods.

Moses, who was educated in the international society of royal Egypt, must have known this Babylonian story. Certain terminology used by Moses in Gen. 1 suggests that he deliberately interacted with it in order to show the truth of the LORD God and His creative activity.

The Hebrew word for day can refer to either a twenty-four-hour period or a period of indefinite length such as in the phrase "day of the LORD" (Joel 1:15; cp. Ps. 90:4; 2 Pet. 3:8). While a twenty-four-hour day has the advantage of narrative simplicity in Gen. 1, the use of "day" in Gen. 2:4 to refer to the entire creative week suggests that Moses might have had something other than six solar days in mind. A definitive understanding of the length of time of Creation remains elusive.

twenty-four-hour days or six periods of time of an indefinite length remains a matter of debate.

The six days of Creation can be grouped into two categories of three days each:

Day 1—light	Day 4—sun, moon, and stars
Day 2—waters beneath waters above (sky)	Day 5—fish, birds
Day 3—dry land, seas and plants	Day 6—animals, people

There is a general correlation between God's creative activities on days one through three and the elements that He created on days four through six. During the first three days, God made the arenas into which the actors of days four through six were placed. Each day built on the previous one, providing what was necessary to sustain life created on the following days.

On day one, God created light. The physical source for this light is a matter of debate, since the sun does not appear until day four. The numerous attempts to explain the light of day one scientifically remain unsatisfactory. This light not only provided the energy needed to sustain life; it indicated that God is a revealer who acts to overcome darkness.

On the second day, God separated the waters of Gen. 1:2 into two regions with the atmosphere, called the "firmament" or "expanse," in between. The waters above the firmament were contained in clouds while the waters below were the surface and subterranean waters of the earth.

On the third day, the surface waters were "gathered together" (perhaps by receding) into seas, lakes, and rivers so that dry land could appear. God then created all manner of plant life, placed by Moses into two general categories of seed-bearing plants and fruit trees. The designation of these specific categories suggests that plants were created to be food for animals and people.

On the fourth day, God created the sun, the moon, and the stars. Moses explains that they were made to provide light (1:15, 17–18) and to be "for signs, and for seasons, and for days and years" (1:14 NASB). This means they were to mark the agricultural calendar, indicating set times to worship God—primary concerns for the Israelites who were entering Canaan.

On the fifth day, God created living beings to inhabit the water and the air. Each fish and bird, like the plants of day three (1:11–12) and the animals of day six (1:24–25), was created "according to its kind" (1:21). This phrase indicates that any natural development of living things that might take place cannot cross the species line. For the first time, God blessed an element of His creation: "Be fruitful and multiply" (1:22 NASB). To be blessed is to enjoy a favored status before God.

The sixth day was the climax of Creation. God first created all land animals: "Beasts of the earth" (wild animals), "cattle" (domesticated animals) and "everything that creeps upon the ground," all "according to their kinds" (1:24–25). These categories of animals are all-inclusive, preventing the natural development of animals across species lines.

Moses compared the coming of God to the light of the rising sun (Deut. 33:2), an image adapted by Isaiah to refer to the Messiah (Isa. 9:1–2; cp. Matt. 4:15–16). Jesus announced that He was the light of the world (John 8:12; 9:5), a theme emphasized by John (John 1:4–5, 9; 3:19; 12:35–36). In Rev. 22:5, John proclaimed that the sun would no longer be needed in the new heaven and earth because "the LORD God will give them light" (NCV)—a clear allusion to the pre-sun source of light in Gen. 1:3.

The Hebrew word "man" in Gen. 1:26 is *'adam*, from which Adam, the first human, takes his personal name. This word for "man" is related to the Hebrew word for "ground," the substance out of which the man was formed (2:7). While *'adam* is often translated by the common noun "man" throughout the Old Testament, in Gen. 1 it is intended to be genderless, or to include both genders. This is clearly stated in Gen. 1:27: "So God created *'adam* in his own image . . . male and female he created them."

For this reason, when *'adam* does not specifically refer to the person Adam in the first chapters of Genesis, it should be translated "mankind" or "human."

Finally, God created people, the crown of His creative work (1:26–31). In a number of ways, Moses clearly distinguishes people from the rest of creation:

1. While God's other creative activities began with the phrase, "Let there be," people were called into existence with the personal command, "Let us make" (1:26).

2. People were created in God's image and likeness (1:26–27) rather than, like the plants and animals, "according to their kind."

3. While the animals were certainly created with gender differences, "male" and "female" are mentioned only in connection with people, indicating the full potential of human relationships (1:27).

4. The blessing bestowed upon people included their right to have responsible dominion over the rest of creation (1:28–30).

Only after people were created did God declare that everything which He had made was "very good."

■ *God carefully and deliberately prepared the*
■ *world to be a special place perfectly suited*
■ *for people. People are to take care of the*
■ *world and have a meaningful relationship*
■ *with their Creator.*

The Seventh Day (2:1–3)

On the seventh day, God rested—not because He was tired but because His work of creation was finished. The description of this day does not end with the formula, "There was evening and there was morning" because the seventh day is unending. Adam and Eve participated in God's "rest" when they were in the Garden of Eden. God continues to enjoy His creation even though it is racked with sin.

Moses used the concluding day of the creation week to introduce the Sabbath, the seventh day of the week during which all Israelites were to abstain from work in order to devote themselves completely to God (Exod. 20:8–11; 31:14).

■ *Sabbath rest is a picture of something*
■ *greater, the fullness of salvation and heaven*
■ *itself (Col. 2:16–17). Someday all of God's*
■ *people will, like God Himself, enter into such*
■ *rest (Heb. 4:1–13).*

The Second Creation Account (2:4–25)

Genesis 1 provides a sequential ordering of the events of Creation while Gen. 2 is topically arranged. For this reason, it is not always easy to mesh the two accounts. But a careful reading shows the general tenor of the two to be the same. This second story of Creation provides details about the creation of people, gives a description of the Garden of Eden, and introduces themes which figure prominently in Gen. 3, the story of the fall of mankind.

Creation of the First Man (2:4–7)

The description of the world before the creation of people which is recorded in Gen. 2:4–6 resembles the early verses of Gen. 1—a land not yet ready for human habitation. There were no "shrubs of the field" or "plants of the field," and "streams" (NIV; KJV "a mist") came up from the earth to water the ground.

The image of God anticipates the Incarnation of Jesus. In Jesus, the God-became-man, God's image was most fully manifest (see Phil. 2:5–8).

The psalmist spoke eloquently of the exalted position of mankind. Psalm 8:5 praises God for making man only "a little lower than the heavenly beings," crowning him with glory and honor and placing all created things under his feet (Ps. 8:5–6). Psalm 139 ponders in awe how people were "skillfully wrought in the depths of the earth" (Ps. 139:15, NASB). It is people who occupy the thoughts of God, and it is for them that He acts (Ps. 40:5).

"*Breathed* is warmly personal, with the face-to-face intimacy of a kiss and the significance that this was giving as well as making; and self-giving at that" (Derek Kidner, *Genesis,* Tyndale Old Testament Commentaries, InterVarsity Press, 1967, p. 60).

The manner in which God created man in Gen. 2:7 is depicted in anthropomorphic terms. God formed man from the dust of the ground and breathed into him the breath of life. The mention of dust emphasizes his creatureliness. It also anticipates the fall of man and his eventual return to the dust from which he was taken (3:19).

Although made in the image of God, Gen. 2:7 assures people that they are not—nor ever will be—divine. At the same time, this verse reveals clearly that people are a unique creation.

Upon receiving the breath of God, man became a "living being" (KJV "living soul"). The Hebrew word which translates "being" in this phrase is related to the idea of "breath" or "to breath." It indicates the transcendent life force present in a being, either animal or human. "Being" and "body" are used in Isa. 10:18 to describe a complete person. In ancient Hebrew thought, a person was an integrated whole: When the "being" was gone, the body died.

■ *People are made from the dust of the ground,*
■ *yet are in the image of God. As such, they are*
■ *created to reach outward and upward.*

The Garden of Eden (2:8–17)

God planted a garden in Eden, an area specially prepared for people to inhabit and enjoy (2:8). It was a place where people had intimate fellowship with God and where they were given every physical thing necessary for life (2:9).

Garden literally means a "protected area." *Eden* means "delight."

In the middle of the garden God planted two special trees—the tree of life and the tree of the knowledge of good and evil. The tree of life appears in Gen. 3:22 and again in Rev. 2:7 and 22:2. The tree of the knowledge of good and evil figures prominently in the story of the fall of man in Gen. 3.

These trees were not intended to have magical qualities but to represent the right which God alone possesses to grant life and to determine what is good and what is not good for mankind. Adam was instructed to care for the garden ("till it and keep it") but not to eat of the fruit of the two trees placed in its center lest he die.

There are significant parallels between Moses' description of the Garden of Eden in Gen. 2 and the tabernacle built under his direction.

In both places, God met man. The gold and onyx (2:12) of Eden anticipate gold and onyx found in the tabernacle furnishings and priestly garments (Exod. 25:1–40; 28:9–20). The Hebrew words translated "till" and "keep" (2:15) are used by Moses to refer to tabernacle "service" (see Num. 3:10) and the "observing" of covenant stipulations (see Deut. 4:6). Eventually the entrance to the Garden was guarded by cherubim (3:24), heavenly beings whose images also adorned the Ark of the Covenant (Exod. 25:19) and the curtains which formed the outside wall of the tabernacle (Exod. 26:1–3).

Moses described the Garden of Eden in a specific way to teach his contemporaries that tabernacle (and later temple) worship was their proper means of approaching God. For Israel, the tabernacle signaled the possibility of entering into an intimate relationship with Him.

Certain motifs in the description of the Garden of Eden have parallels in ancient Near Eastern myth. Mesopotamian literary documents are fascinated with the lush garden of the gods where divine beings dwell in opulence and ease. Sacred trees often appear in ancient Near Eastern art, but it is unclear whether such trees were seen as trees of life. In the Babylonian Gilgamesh Epic, a tale which includes a flood story often compared to Gen. 6–9, the hero finds a plant at the bottom of the sea guaranteed to give eternal life, but he quickly loses it to a water serpent.

Scholars have long tried to identify the location of the Garden of Eden. Of the four rivers mentioned which flow out of the garden, two are well known—the Tigris and Euphrates flow from the Zagros and Taurus Mountains through modern Iraq (ancient Mesopotamia) into the Persian Gulf. The Pishon is unknown, although recent satellite imagery has identified a dry riverbed in north central Saudi Arabia flowing into the Persian Gulf. Some Bible students suggest this might have been that river. The fourth river, the Gihon, flows around the land of Cush (perhaps Ethiopia) but bears the same name as the small spring which gushes out of the hill on which Jerusalem is built.

Medieval stories placed the Garden of Eden on the island of Ceylon (modern Sri Lanka) east of India. Many persons today locate the garden in northern Iraq or under the northern extremity of the Persian Gulf.

The Garden of Eden was made as a home for people to live in the way they were meant to live, and to delight in a close relationship with God. To eat of the trees in the middle of the garden would be to claim rights that belonged only to God and hence break the relationship that man was created to enjoy.

Companionship: The First Woman (2:18–25)

The climactic event of Gen. 1 was the creation of man, male and female (1:27). The climactic event of Gen. 2 was the completion of man/male—by the creation of his female companion.

The man first exercised his God-given right of dominion over creation by giving names to the animals (2:19–20). None of the animals provided suitable companionship for him. This was another sign of his uniqueness.

- *God took the woman from the man's skeletal*
- *structure to show that the two were made to*
- *be perfectly compatible. The man could now*
- *enjoy an intimate and fulfilling relationship*
- *with another human being.*

QUESTIONS TO GUIDE YOUR STUDY

1. What does the way in which God created the world tell us about Him?

2. According to Gen. 1–2, why did God create people?

3. How does Gen. 1–2 teach the uniqueness of both man and woman?

THE FALL AND ITS CONSEQUENCES (3:1–6:8)

Genesis continues with a story that rapidly brings the conditions of Eden to a close. This is followed by an account of the spread of sin, from generation to generation, throughout the world.

The First Sin (3:1–24)

The first two chapters of Genesis focus on goodness and life. Chapter 3 provides the answer for the question, Why is there evil and death? How can evil be reconciled with God's goodness and the fact that everything originated with Him?

The Origin of Sin (3:1–7)

The origin of sin is found in the choice of the man and woman to obey the voice of the serpent rather than the voice of God. The serpent, speaking briefly and only twice, caused the woman to doubt first God's word (3:1) and then God's goodness (3:4–5).

The focus of the serpent's beguiling speech was subtle: the tree of the knowledge of good and evil must have been intended by God to keep knowledge of good and evil from people. But people, created in God's image, need this knowledge to be like Him. By placing the tree off limits, God had declared that the ability and right to know what was good and what was not good for people was something that He had reserved for Himself.

The woman, enticed by the serpent (cp. 2 Cor. 11:3), ate of the tree and in turn gave some of its fruit to the man, who ate willingly. In flaunting God's right to know and trying to be wise in their own eyes (3:6), the man and woman decided that they no longer needed God.

The only proper companion for a one-of-a-kind being is another being like it. This is the gist of the phrase, "Helper suitable for him" (2:18). *Helper* is a word often used to describe God's activity on behalf of people (see Exod. 18:4; Pss. 70:5; 121:1–2; 124:8), thereby giving the word great dignity. "Suitable for him" (literally "like that which is in front of him") implies an equality of essence and compatibility.

The woman was made from the man's "rib" or side while he was deep in sleep. In this way the mystery of creation was preserved for the man; he could claim no active role in the fulfilling of his need for companionship.

Moses understood that the family, as an institution ordained by God from creation, was to be based on a monogamous relationship between a man and a woman (2:24; cp. Matt. 19:5; Mark 10:7–8; 1 Cor. 6:16; Eph. 5:31). The man and woman of Eden—Adam and Eve—formed the prototype family. Their mutual commitment created a new entity, "one flesh."

The creation story ends with a note that the man and woman were both naked but not ashamed (2:25). Unlike today, nakedness among the Hebrews did not carry connotations of embarrassment or sexual titillation. Rather, nakedness indicated shame for previous sin (Gen. 9:20–23; Isa. 3:17; 20:2–4; 47:2–3; Jer. 13:22–26). Before there was sin, there could be no shame, and both nakedness and sexuality were undefiled. Together, Adam and Eve experienced perfect communion, knowing well their God-given sameness and differences.

Genesis offers no explanation as to where this particular serpent came from, nor is the serpent specifically called Satan (literally "adversary") in this account. Even though the ultimate source of evil is not explained in Genesis, two facts are clear: evil did not originate with God, and it is subject to His power and will.

- *Created to be free and exalted beings, people*
- *have the capacity to choose God or to reject*
- *Him. Beginning with Adam and because of*
- *Adam, all people have chosen to elevate their*
- *own desires over the desires of God.*

The Judgment on Sin (3:8–19)

God sought fellowship with Adam and Eve while "walking in the garden in the cool of the day." But upon hearing Him, the man and woman fled into a self-imposed exile. God then questioned the man and the woman about their loss of innocence (3:11). The man blamed God (3:12), and the woman blamed the serpent (3:13). God responded by pronouncing a judgment which impaired the blessings He had established at Creation.

The judgment placed on the serpent was called a "curse" (3:14). The serpent was consigned to a life of crawling on his belly (3:14). This judgment was not intended to explain a biological characteristic of snakes but to indicate the humiliation and eventual defeat of Satan—the one embodied in the serpent.

The woman's ability to be "fruitful and multiply" (1:28) would be accompanied by pain (3:16), and the "one flesh" relationship which she enjoyed with her husband (2:24) would be subject to the strain of competing wills (3:16).

The man would have to toil for a living (3:17, 19; cp. 2:15) because the ground, which had naturally produced plants for food (1:29–30) was cursed to grow thorns and thistles (3:17–18). Ultimately he was to die (3:19).

- People, created in the image of God, succumbed to the temptation to become even more like God than they already were (3:5).
- As a result, they would share the dust of the serpent (3:14, 19). But someday the Messiah would come to defeat sin and bring people back into a right relationship with God.

The Consequences of Sin (3:20–24)

After God's pronouncements, the man and woman tried to get on with their lives. Adam named his wife "Eve," a word related to the Hebrew word for "life," because "she was the mother of all the living" (3:20 NASB). God provided clothing for Adam and Eve, physically covering their shame, by killing animals (3:21). Finally, Adam and Eve were exiled from Eden (3:22–24)—a physical portrayal of their spiritual separation from God.

They fled from their home toward the east (3:24), as would their son, Cain, following his sin (4:16). Many years later, Abraham would leave the east (Mesopotamia), following the call of God to a land which He had again prepared for His people (11:31–12:3).

Old Testament writers understood the corrupting effect of sin on humanity (Jer. 17:9). But it was the apostle Paul who most clearly set out the doctrine of original sin. Paul noted that sin had entered the world and spread to all people because of the sin of one man (Rom. 5:12). He drew a comparison between Adam—the one who had originally been without sin—and Jesus who—although also without sin—was punished for the sin of Adam (Rom. 5:14–21).

The curse on the serpent was messianic in nature. God announced to the serpent—no doubt within earshot of Adam and Eve—that while the serpent would bruise the heel of the woman's "seed," her "seed" would crush the serpent's head (3:15). All Christians understand this to be a reference to Jesus, the woman's descendant who was harmed by Satan at the Cross but who will ultimately destroy the evil one.

The destiny of Satan is described in the New Testament in terms of "falling down." After the seventy who were sent throughout Galilee to announce the coming of Jesus had returned to Him, Jesus proclaimed, "I saw Satan fall like lightning from heaven" (Luke 10:18). Just before His crucifixion, Jesus declared, "Now the ruler of this world shall be cast out" (John 12:31, NASB). The Book of Revelation relates a threefold falling of Satan: onto the earth (12:9), into the abyss (20:1–3), and finally into the lake of fire (20:10). All of these fallings are anticipated in God's pronouncement in Eden that the serpent would "bite the dust" (3:14).

■ *All sinners must face the consequences of*
■ *their sin, and the primary consequence is*
■ *separation from God.*

The Spread of Sin (4:1–6:8)

After entering the world, sin quickly polluted all of humanity. Adam's first two sons were murderer and murder victim, and his family was burdened with the consequences. Each succeeding generation became entrapped by its own evil desires until at last God "grieved that he had made man on the earth, and his heart was filled with pain" (6:6).

Cain and Abel (4:1–26)

The story of Cain and Abel, well known in Western thought and literature, set the stage for sin's advance. The acclaimed playwright Arthur Miller said, "If a brother could murder a brother, nobody is safe, all bets are off, and there is no future" (David Rosenberg, ed., *Genesis: As It Is Written*, [HarperSanFrancisco, 1996], p. 37). But God graciously provided a future, even in the darkness of Gen. 4.

THE FIRST MURDER (4:1–16)

Eve thought her firstborn son would be the promised seed of Gen. 3:15 who would destroy the serpent and set everything aright. Upon his birth, she declared, "With the help of the LORD I have brought forth a man" (4:1).

"Cain" is a play on the Hebrew verb *brought forth*. The name of her next son, Abel, was not explained by Eve, but it means "vapor" or "breath-like" and carries forward the ominous tone of Gen. 3.

Cain, a farmer, and Abel, a shepherd, brought offerings to the LORD. God accepted Abel's offering but "did not look with favor" on that of Cain, prompting Cain to kill his brother (4:8).

Some interpreters conclude that the reason God accepted Abel's gift was that it was a blood sacrifice, but this is not indicated in the text. Moses, who had received God's instructions regarding blood sacrifices on Mt. Sinai, could have called Abel's gift a "blood sacrifice," but instead he labeled the gifts of both Abel and Cain as "offerings" (4:3–5). The acceptability of their gifts lay not in a ceremonial act but in their heart attitude.

The integrity of Abel's heart is seen in his willingness to offer the best of what he had to God (4:4), while Cain's heart was characterized by envy and resentment (4:5; cp. 1 John 3:12).

Unlike his parents, Cain showed no remorse for his sin. His arrogant retort to God, "Am I my brother's keeper?" (4:9) demonstrated that he was not even his brother's brother. Cain was "cursed" (4:11), a judgment even his parents did not receive. God then banished Cain into exile, graciously marking him for protection from the wild (4:12, 15).

■ *The murder of Abel by Cain shows how*
■ *quickly sin takes over a human life. God*
■ *judges people according to their heart atti-*
■ *tude.*

CAIN'S LEGACY (4:17–24)

The story of the first murder is followed by a genealogical narrative (the "Cainite genealogy"). Six generations descending from Cain are mentioned, ending with the sons of Lamech, from whom various aspects of civilization developed, including animal husbandry (4:20), the arts (4:21), and technology (4:22).

Mosaic legislation instituted numerous physical acts regulating Israel's formal access to God. Many of these involved offerings or sacrifices. Cereal, grain, and peace offerings were offered to God in praise and thanksgiving for blessings which He had bestowed (Lev. 2:1–3:17). Burnt, sin, trespass, and guilt offerings were demanded by God on the occasion of sin (Lev. 1:3–17; 4:1–7:10). Not all sins required blood sacrifice. The Old Testament is clear that people were forgiven not because of their outward acts of sacrifice but because acts of sacrifice were to represent their penitent heart before God (1 Sam. 15:22; Ps. 51:16–17; Isa. 1:12–17; cp. Heb. 10:4).

gation

Abel is a tragic figure. While the Bible does not say much about him, we can see in Abel the full potential of youth cut off in its prime. Abel was righteous—"such a good boy," we would say—but was killed suddenly, without warning, and through not the slightest fault of his own. The psalmist cried out that life sometimes seems vaporous: "Each man's life is but a breath!" (Ps. 39:5, 11); the Hebrew word he used for "breath" was *abel*.

The Bible does not say where Cain got his wife (4:17). The traditional view that he married his sister is found in the book of Jubilees, a Jewish apocalyptic (visionary) work from the second century B.C., which mentions that Cain married his sister 'Awan (Jubilees 4:1).

The genealogy of Cain ends with the "song of the sword," a boast by Lamech that he "killed a man for wounding me" (4:23). Lamech's act of murder was different from Cain's—he was physically provoked and maybe even acted out of self-defense. Yet his gloating and eagerness to be avenged "seventy-seven fold" marks the rampage of evil. Cain's legacy had some positive effects, but the advances of human civilization could not solve the problem of sin.

■ *The solution for the world's problems lies not*
■ *with human advancement, but with God.*

A RIGHTEOUS LINE (4:25–26)
Having traced the line of Cain, Moses returned to Adam and Eve, who were now the same as childless. Eve counted on her next son, Seth, being a replacement for Abel (4:25). Seth named his son Enosh, another Hebrew word which, like Adam (*'adam*), means "mankind." In effect, Enosh was a new Adam, for in his days "men began to call on the name of the LORD" (4:26).

■ *The line of Seth plays a dominant role in*
■ *Genesis, producing Noah and all who came*
■ *after him.*

The Descendants of Adam (5:1–6:8)
Having carefully portrayed the creation of the world, the character of God, the nature of mankind, and the fundamental evil of sin, the biblical story now quickly advances. Ten generations, from Adam to Noah, unfold in little more than a chapter. When God speaks again, it is to re-create the world that He had made (6:7).

TEN MEN OF NAME (5:1–32)

The genealogy in Gen. 5 is called the Sethite genealogy because it lists the descendants of Seth. It begins with a reminder of Creation (5:1) and of blessing (5:2). Adam was made in the likeness and image of God; Seth was born in the likeness and image of Adam (5:3). In this way, God is seen as the Father of all mankind and especially of the chosen line of Abraham (12:2–3).

The Sethite genealogy contains ten names. Each entry ends with the words "and he died," sounding as a bell tolling the effects of sin (2:17; 3:19) across the annals of history. The blessing of God and the curse of sin are passed from generation to generation.

Moses used the phrase "walking with God" to depict the righteous life lived in obedience to the Torah, God's law (Deut. 30:15–16). It would be a mistake to equate Moses' understanding of "walking with God" with a legalistic obedience to the Law. Certain standards of behavior are to be expected from a true follower of God, and the Mosaic legislation provided those for ancient Israel. Adam, Enoch, Noah, and Abraham all lived before the Law was given to Moses; yet, Moses himself took care to describe their lives as "walking with God."

Enoch, the seventh name in the genealogy, breaks the formulaic pattern (5:21–24). The concluding phrase "and he died" is conspicuously absent. Instead, we read that "Enoch walked with God; then he was no more, because God took him away" (5:24). One man, in the midst of many, was faithful and did not die (Heb. 11:5).

■ *"Walking" with God is a metaphor that Moses*
■ *used to describe the intimate relationship*
■ *which God had enjoyed with Adam and Eve in*
■ *the Garden of Eden (3:8). Enoch (5:24), Noah*
■ *(6:9), and Abraham (17:1) all "walked with*
■ *God," living in ways that were pleasing to Him.*

By using this phrase, Moses intended to depict that a relationship based on faith and trust was superior to a relationship based on external actions.

THE SONS OF GOD AND THE DAUGHTERS OF MEN (6:1–4)

The Sethite genealogy ends with two short narratives. The first recounts the intermarriage of "sons of God" with "daughters of men" (6:1–4).

There have been several attempts to explain the long life spans of the men who appear in Gen. 5. But none of these explanations enjoy universal acceptance: (1) The numbers should be taken literally, indicating that the great physical vitality which was present at Creation only gradually diminished; (2) the life spans were calculated on a base-6 mathematical system used in ancient Mesopotamia rather than on today's base-10 system; (3) the genealogy is made to resemble various Sumerian and Babylonian king lists which give high numbers for the reigns of their pre-Flood monarchs; (4) each number represents not the life span of an individual but that of his family line.

Because this episode occurs just before the story of the Flood, most interpreters read it as portraying a specific example of the kinds of sin which brought God's judgment. There are two traditional views on this sin.

The first view holds that the "sons of God" were angels (now fallen) and the "daughters of men" were humans. The ensuing marriage between divine and human beings broke God's created boundaries to such a degree that He had to destroy all of creation. While the term *sons of God* is used later in the Old Testament only to refer to angels (Job 1:6; 2:1; 38:7; Pss. 29:1; 89:7), its meaning as "angels" in Gen. 6 is far from certain. The marriage of angels and people would give Genesis a mythological tone.

The second view holds that the "sons of God" were godly people (such as from the line of Seth), while the "daughters of men" were ungodly people (such as from the line of Cain). In this case, the sin would be the marriage of believers and unbelievers. This view, which was held by Luther and Calvin, is more attractive to most believers.

- *The marriage of the sons of God with daugh-*
- *ters of men was typical of the kind of evil*
- *which led to God's judgment through the*
- *Flood.*

WORLDWIDE WICKEDNESS (6:5–8)

The final narrative before the story of the Flood offers both despair and hope. The earth, created to be a home in which man and God would walk and talk together, had become the arena for unbridled wickedness. Man, made in the image of God and at one time innocent, was totally corrupt (6:5). And God, who had rested in pleasant satisfaction after Creation, was grieved with pain (6:6).

God's response was to "de-create." By His word—the same power which brought the universe into existence—God announced His intent to destroy all living things (6:7). He named the creatures which He would destroy in the reverse order of their creation: people, then animals, then creeping things, then birds (cp. 1:26, 24, 20; Zeph. 1:3).

But the last word, as is often the case in a biblical passage (see 2 Kings 25:27–30; 2 Chron. 36:22–23; Amos 9:13–15), is one of hope: "But Noah found favor in the eyes of the LORD" (6:8). One man and his family (6:10) were chosen to provide the way out. Through him, God began to re-create the world and His people.

Genesis 6:1–4 shows the inevitable and inexorable moral decline which results from what the apostle Paul called being "unequally yoked with unbelievers" (2 Cor. 6:14). The concern to marry well is repeated in the patriarchal history section of Genesis thus showing that it was an important theme throughout the book (24:1–4; 28:1; cp. Gen. 19:14; 26:34–35; 27:46).

■ *Sin quickly spreads from generation to gen-*
■ *eration. Eventually God has to judge sin, but*
■ *He graciously provides a way of escape for*
■ *those who walk with Him.*

QUESTIONS TO GUIDE YOUR STUDY

1. What did Adam and Eve do wrong in the Garden of Eden?

2. How did the punishment of Adam and Eve change God's previous blessing? To what were they condemned?

3. How do the early chapters of Genesis teach us what it means to "walk with God?"

Noah's ark had three decks and was 450 feet long, 75 feet wide and 45 feet high. It had a displacement of forty thousand tons. This was a huge boat for ancient times, but it was of relatively modest size when compared to today's large cargo ships.

"Noah found favor in the eyes of the LORD" (6:8). The Hebrew word which is here translated "favor" means charm, elegance, or grace, and is used most often in nonreligious contexts in the Bible (for example, "gracious speech"—Prov. 22:11, or a "kindhearted" woman—Prov. 11:16, NIV). The focus of the word is on the positive qualities of the person or thing receiving the attribute of favor.

While Noah was a sinner, he was also—in comparison to those around him—"blameless" (6:9). We should not deny God's sovereignty and His right to choose whomever He wills. But His choice of Noah rested at least in part in Noah's openness to the things of God.

THE FLOOD AND ITS CONSEQUENCES (6:9–10:32)

The Flood is the third great event of the primeval history section of Genesis. The themes already introduced in Genesis—creation, blessing, sin, judgment, grace—are magnified through the prism of the flood waters. After the Flood, God established an everlasting covenant with all living creatures on the earth (9:16). In spite of this covenant, the human tendency toward sin did not change (9:20–27).

The Destruction of the World (6:9–7:24)

The opening episode of this account is the destruction of the world under a chaotic deluge of water.

Anticipation of the Flood (6:9–12)

Genesis 6:9–12 forms an introduction to the story of the Flood. Noah is described in three ways: he was "righteous," he was "blameless among the people of his time," and, like Enoch, he "walked with God" (6:9). Taken together, these descriptions set Noah in sharp contrast to the violent and corrupt nature of his contemporaries (6:11–12; cp. Matt. 24:37–39; Heb. 11:7; 2 Pet. 2:5).

■ *In the midst of impending judgment, God chose*
■ *to save the only righteous person on earth.*

Preparation for the Flood (6:13–7:5)

In order to prepare Noah for the Flood, God gave him two commands. The first was to build an ark of sufficient size to hold himself, his family (6:18; eight persons total), one pair of every animal (6:19–20), and plenty of food for all (6:21). This Noah did (6:22).

God's command to build the ark included the announcement that He was about to destroy "every creature that has the breath of life in it" (6:17). Noah and his family, however, were to be saved through the ark because God was establishing His covenant with them (6:18). This covenant would be ratified with Noah and his descendants after the floodwaters went down (9:9–10).

The second command given to Noah was to enter the ark with seven pairs of every clean animal (7:1–3). This Noah also did (7:5). The concern for clean animals in the days of Noah—long before Mosaic legislation regulated ritual cleanness and uncleanness among the Israelites (Lev. 10:10; 11:1–47)—is unexpected. After the waters receded, Noah offered a burnt offering of clean animals to the LORD (8:20).

Noah's ark and the basket in which Moses was placed as an infant (Exod. 2:3) are identified by the same term in Hebrew. This suggests that there are important parallels between the stories of Noah and baby Moses: (1) Both arks were made of wood covered by bitumen; (2) both Noah and Moses were delivered from certain death by floating in the water; (3) because Noah and Moses were saved, both preserved an entire people; (4) as adults, both received God's covenant.

Moses clearly intended to tell his audience that like Noah, he—and they—were beginning a new epoch in God's redemptive history.

■ *Noah proved his righteousness by obeying*
■ *God's command to build an ark. His obedi-*
■ *ence provided an example of faith for the*

The word *righteous* is used most often in the Bible to indicate that a person has met an established standard of right conduct. In the Old Testament, that standard was usually the Mosaic law (see Deut. 4:8; Ps. 1:2), but it could be any command given by God. Noah's righteousness became evident when he obeyed God's command to build and enter the ark (6:22; 7:5, 9, 16).

The word *blameless* has as its primary connotation moral purity and integrity (Deut. 18:13). Abraham was described in the same way as Noah (Gen. 15:6; 17:1), indicating that he was also God's chosen instrument to restore a disintegrating world.

Noah's flood penetrated the consciousness of the biblical writers. The Old Testament poets often used deep water as an image for overwhelming trouble (Ps. 69:1, 14–15; Isa. 8:7–8; Lam. 3:54), and even death (Jon. 2:5–6).

It is impossible to determine the exact date of the Flood since conclusive archaeological and geological evidence is lacking.

Archaeologists have determined that ancient Mesopotamian cities such as Ur and Kish were periodically inundated by floods during the fourth and third millenniums B.C., burying whole buildings with thick layers of mud and silt. However, these flood layers cannot be identified with Noah's flood because they date to a wide range of time periods.

The archaeological record offers only enough evidence to conclude that after the eighth millennium B.C., no single flood disrupted civilization throughout the ancient world.

■ *Israelites of Moses' day just as it does for us*
■ *(Heb. 11:7).*

The Coming of the Flood (7:6–24)

The account of the floodwater inundating the earth is both majestic and terrible. Moses was careful to describe the Flood in terms reminiscent of the Creation. Like Gen. 1, the account of the Flood is structured by a careful counting of the days:

- 7 days of waiting for the waters to come (7:4, 10),
- 40 days of waters rising (7:12, 17),
- 150 days of waters prevailing (7:24; 8:3),
- 40 days of waters receding (8:6),
- 7 days of waiting for the waters to recede (8:10), and
- 7 more days of waiting for the waters to recede completely (8:12).

The animals preserved on the ark parallel those created in Gen. 1: beasts, cattle, creeping things, and birds, each according to their kind (6:20; 7:14–16). It was not just the world but creation itself which was destroyed. With the flood, the earth returned to its watery primordial state.

■ *Through the Flood, God "de-created" the*
■ *world that He had made. Under water, the*
■ *world was no longer suitable for human habi-*
■ *tation.*

The Re-creation of the World (8:1–9:19)

After destroying the world, God carefully restored it. He then established a covenant with Noah, the new Adam, and with all living creatures, promising that He would never again destroy the world by a flood.

The End of the Flood (8:1–19)

Slowly the floodwaters receded. After the ark had come to rest on Mt. Ararat, Noah sent out a raven, then a dove, three times (8:7–12). When the dove did not return, Noah knew the waters had receded enough so everyone could leave the ark (8:18–19).

Moses continued to use creation language to describe the waters receding from the earth:

1. Twice Moses called the floodwaters the "deep" (7:11; 8:2), the same term he used to characterize the not-yet-ready earth in Gen. 1:2.
2. God then sent a "wind" blowing over the earth to dissipate the flood waters (8:1) so dry land on which people could live would appear (8:3–5). The same Hebrew word, translated "Spirit," moved over the face of the deep in Gen. 1:2.
3. Noah removed the covering of the ark on the first day of the first month of the new year—a time fitting the beginning of a new world. God then spoke (cp. 1:24), and the earth was repopulated.
4. Noah was told to "bring forth" (cp. 1:24) the living creatures from the ark so they could "be fruitful and multiply" on the earth (cp. 1:22).

As God commanded, so Noah did (8:18). All living creatures left the ark "by families" (8:19). This is a warm term anticipating a future blessing which God would make to all the human families of the earth (12:3).

■ *After the Flood, God re-created the world.*
■ *Carefully and deliberately, just as He did at*

31

The extent of Noah's flood has been hotly debated. The Genesis account itself points to a cataclysmic flood of worldwide proportions (7:19–23). In addition, flood stories found among peoples from across the world—Africans, Persians, Indians, Australians, Melanesians, Eskimos, and Native Americans—suggest a common experience. Those who accept a more limited flood hold that the biblical account must be read from the perspective of its original audience. In this way, the flood needed to affect only the known, inhabited world. Because the archaeological and geological evidence for the flood is inconclusive, the extent of the flood remains a matter of faith.

The word used for *rainbow* was simply "bow," the same word that refers to the weapon of war. By using this word, God indicated that His covenant with Noah was a covenant of peace and that He was laying down His bow in victory.

■ *creation, God again prepared a place where*
■ *His people could live.*

God's Covenant with Noah (8:20–9:19)

In his first recorded act after leaving the ark, Noah built an altar to the LORD and offered on it a burnt offering of clean animals and birds that had survived the flood (8:20). Noah's sacrifice, like that of Abel (cp. 4:4), was pleasing to God (8:21).

God then resolved that, even though "every inclination of [man's] heart is evil from childhood" (8:21) and would certainly stand in need of future judgment, the ground would never again be cursed for man's misdeeds (8:21–22). In this way, the blessing which God had placed on the earth at Creation was reestablished (cp. Deut. 11:12). The basis for the Flood (6:5) had become the basis for God's grace after the Flood (8:21).

God also blessed people again. In words echoing the Creation, God commanded Noah and his sons to "be fruitful and multiply" (9:1, 7; cp. 1:28) and have dominion over the earth (9:2; cp. 1:28). As at Creation, God provided Noah and his family with food. This time God allowed people to eat animals (9:3; cp. 1:29) with the exception that "you must not eat meat that has its lifeblood still in it" (9:4).

God told Noah there was to be an accounting for every violation of human life. Because man was made in the image of God, one who kills another must himself be killed (9:5–6). This established the principle of *lex talionis* ("an eye for an eye") found in the Mosaic legislation (see Exod. 21:23–25).

Finally, God established His covenant with Noah and his descendants. This covenant was both universal (9:9–10, 17), eternal (9:12, 16), and unconditional. Through His covenant, God formally announced that He would never again destroy the entire earth with a flood (9:11). The covenant was sealed with the sign of a rainbow (9:13; cp. 9:14, 16).

A covenant formed a bond between two parties. A covenant between nations signaled peace and an alliance of mutual friendship and support (see Gen. 14:13; Josh. 9:16). A covenant between families meant that members of one family would treat members of the other as their own (Gen. 31:44). A covenant between a monarch and his subjects bound the monarch to protect and provide for his subjects while they were to obey their king.

The ratification of a covenant typically included signs and oaths that promised blessings for obedience and curses for disobedience.

- *The covenant that God established with*
- *Noah signaled that God would again seek to*
- *establish a relationship with people. His pro-*
- *vision after the Flood included the notion of*
- *blood atonement, a principle which is exem-*
- *plified in the death of Jesus.*

The Reemergence of Sin (9:20–29)

The story of Noah ends with an episode that is a little unsettling but thoroughly realistic. Noah planted a vineyard, drank wine made from its grapes, and then fell asleep, drunk and naked, in his tent (9:20–21). His son Ham saw what had happened but did nothing except tell his

God is in the business of giving second chances. The world of Noah's day deserved to be destroyed, and it was. But with the passing of the Flood, everything became new again. Everyone who puts his or her trust in Jesus receives a second chance at life: "Therefore, if anyone is in Christ he is a new creation; the old has gone, the new has come!" (2 Cor. 5:17).

Because of the close connection between blood and life, blood was to have a higher purpose than simply serve as food for mankind. Mosaic legislation instituted a means of sacrificial atonement for sins: by shedding the blood of an animal, man's own blood did not need to be shed as punishment for his wrongdoing. This is the essence of what theologians call substitutionary atonement.

The writer of Hebrews teaches that Jesus abolished the Old Testament sacrificial system since His death was a once-for-all act of substitution on behalf of sinful people (Heb. 9:11–28).

brothers, Shem and Japheth, who covered their father (9:22–23). When Noah awoke, he cursed Canaan, Ham's son, for his father's misdeeds but blessed Shem and Japheth (9:24–27).

This story is reminiscent of life in the Garden of Eden. Noah fell in his own garden and ended up, like Adam, naked and shamed. His sons, echoing Cain and Abel, reacted differently. Ham treated sin lightly. In telling his brothers of Noah's condition, Ham failed to honor his father. This is considered a serious breach of Middle Eastern etiquette, even today. Shem and Japheth acted righteously by dealing with Noah's sin in a dignified and proper manner.

In response to their actions, Noah blessed both Shem and Japheth. Of the two, Shem received a more favored position (9:26–27). It was from Shem's line that Abraham (11:10–27) and his descendants, the Israelites, would come.

Ham, however, disqualified himself from God's blessing and was instead cursed through his son, Canaan. The mention of Canaan rather than Ham was significant for the Israelites of Moses' day who were about to enter the land of Canaan. As Canaan was made subservient to his brothers (uncles) by Noah (9:25), so the Canaanites were to be subdued (but not enslaved) by the Israelites (cp. Deut. 31:3).

This curse in no way suggests that the line of Ham was ethnically inferior to the descendants of Shem or Japheth. The Canaanites were destroyed by Joshua because their social and religious practices threatened to corrupt the faith of Israel (Josh. 23:12–13). God warned Israel that if they turned from Him, they would be punished in the manner of the Canaanites (Deut. 29:16–28).

- Even after the Flood, persons who were as
- righteous as Noah could not by themselves
- maintain the blessings which God had given
- them. God's choice of the line of Shem over
- his brothers gave Shem both privilege and
- responsibility—a challenge which the
- descendants of Shem seldom lived up to.

Both racism and bigotry are abhorred by God and condemned by the Bible. All people are created in the image of God and are of equal value to Him (Gen. 1:26–27; Ps. 8:3–8). God's choice of Seth and then Shem to beget a people who would stand in special relationship to Him (Exod. 19:5) was never intended to segregate Israel from the world or instill in them feelings of superiority.

Jesus and the Apostles broke down the Jews' self-imposed racial, ethnic, and national barriers between themselves and others (Gal. 3:28–29). Following their lead, all Christians have the responsibility to embrace all peoples for the sake of the Gospel.

The Reaffirmation of God's Blessing (10:1–32)

The result of God's command to "be fruitful and multiply and fill the earth" (9:1, NASB; cp. 1:28) can be seen in Gen. 10. This chapter is often titled "the table of nations" because it provides a listing of nations (or people groups—cp. 10:5, 20, 31) which inhabited the earth in the days before Abraham. It also gives a general description of that portion of the ancient world in which they lived.

By including the table of nations in the primeval history section of Genesis, Moses showed that God, the Creator of the earth and "father" of Adam (5:1–3; cp. Luke 3:38), is concerned about all the world's people.

Genesis 10 takes the form of a genealogy. It is divided into three sections according to the three sons of Noah: Shem, Ham, and Japheth (10:1). While not all of the names can be identified with certainty, the general division of the land into three major ethnic groups is clear.

The Sons of Japheth (10:1–5)

The nations connected to Japheth inhabited the area from the Caspian Sea through southeastern Europe to the Mediterranean basin and perhaps as far west as Spain (Tarshish?). When the Old

Testament poets and prophets spoke of the universal kingdom of God, they did so in terms of these peoples and lands (see Ps. 72:8–11; Isa. 41:1; 42:10; 49:1; Ezek. 38:2). It was primarily into this area that the New Testament church spread under the ministry of Paul.

The Sons of Ham (10:6–20)

The nations connected to Ham inhabited northeastern Africa, the western coast of the Arabian peninsula, and the Fertile Crescent from Egypt into Mesopotamia. Some of these nations figured prominently in the biblical story as enemies of Israel, particularly Egypt, Babel (Babylon), and Canaan.

The Sons of Shem (10:21–32)

The nations connected to Shem inhabited the eastern lands: modern Iraq, Iran, and eastern Saudi Arabia. The genealogy of Shem split at the sons of Eber (10:25); the descendants of his son Joktan are given in Gen. 10, while the descendants of his other son Peleg are found in Gen. 11. It was Peleg's line which led to Abraham (11:18–26) and eventually the Israelites.

■ *God's concern for the nations caused Him to*
■ *choose one line, that of Shem, through which*
■ *He would reveal Himself in a special way*
■ *and eventually bless nations of the world.*

QUESTIONS TO GUIDE YOUR STUDY

1. How does the biblical description of the Flood remind the reader of Genesis about the Creation? Why is this connection important?

2. How does the life of Noah illustrate what it means to be faithful and what it means to be sinful?

3. What is the importance of the table of nations for the biblical story?

THE CONFUSION AT BABEL AND ITS CONSEQUENCES (11:1–26)

The incident at the tower of Babel is the last great event of the primeval history section of Genesis. The focus of the story is not the tower, which many readers emphasize, but the attempt of people to gain power for themselves at the expense of God. The genealogy that follows narrows the focus of attention from the misdeeds of the nations to the obedience of one man.

The Tower of Babel (11:1–9)

Genesis 11 reports that as men migrated eastward they found a plain in the land of Shinar where they set about to build a city and a tower "whose top will reach into heaven" (11:2–4, NASB). Their motive was to "make a name for [them]selves" lest they be scattered across the earth (11:4). God "came down" from heaven to see the city and tower (11:5); while large to them, it was tiny in His eyes.

God's response was to scatter the builders by confusing their language (11:6–8). The city with its tower, which remained unfinished, was called "Babel," a play on the Hebrew verb "to confuse" (11:9). Babel is also the Hebrew name for Babylon.

The reason why God stopped the work on the city and tower must be found in the builder's attempt to establish unity and identity through their own efforts. The builders of Babel sought to establish their own religious and social structures. The phrase, "So that we may make a name

Most interpreters believe the tower of Gen. 11:4 was a ziggurat. A ziggurat was a large temple tower shaped somewhat like a pyramid but with its sides recessed at intervals. At the base and the top of the ziggurat were temples where images of the city's deities were kept and religious ceremonies were held at significant times throughout the year. The entire structure was made of mud bricks. Archaeologists have found several ziggurats in southern Mesopotamia cities, including Babylon; the best preserved is at Ur. The Babylonians called their ziggurat "the temple of the foundation of heaven and earth."

The land of Shinar is identified with the section of southern Mesopotamia where the Tigris and Euphrates rivers flow in relatively close proximity to one another. Archaeologists have determined that before the fourth millennium B.C. this region was largely uninhabited because it was too swampy. As the area dried, it became an ideal location for urban centers to develop.

During the fourth millennium B.C., numerous large cities were built in southern Mesopotamia along the Tigris and Euphrates. One of these, Babylon (Gen 10:10; 11:9), eventually gave its name to the entire region (Babylonia).

for ourselves" (11:4), indicates self-empowerment coupled with national fame and prestige, both of which are forms of rebellion against the God of creation.

The story of the tower of Babel is really the story of the founding of the city of Babylon. In the Bible, the city of Babylon is the paradigm of gentile pride and wickedness (cp. Isa. 13:1–14:27; 47:1–15; Jer. 50:1–51:64; cp. Ps. 137:1–9). For the biblical writers, Babylon represented everything that stood against God and His blessings for mankind.

■ *The founding of Babylonia and its capital city*
■ *Babylon represented a form of rebellion against*
■ *God because it involved pagan religious and*
■ *social systems. It was out of Babylonia (Ur of the*
■ *Chaldees) that God would call Abraham, and it*
■ *was a type of spiritual Babylonia from which*
■ *God sought to keep Abraham's descendants.*

The Family of Shem (11:10–26)

The primeval history section of Genesis ends with the genealogy of Shem. Ten generations are given, ending with the sons of Terah: Abram, Nahor, and Haran.

The effects of Babel were overcome in a graphic way at Pentecost as the Jerusalem Jews miraculously understood the speech of persons from across the known world (Acts 2:5–13).

The genealogies in the early chapters of Genesis serve to direct the attention of the reader to God's chosen line, the line from which the "seed" promised to Eve would come (3:15). Of the three sons of Adam, the line of Seth was chosen (5:1–31). Of the three sons of Noah, the line of Shem was chosen (10:1; 11:10–26). Now, of the three sons of Terah, the line of Abram (Abraham) will be chosen (11:26; 12:1–3). The hope of God's promise to His people continues.

Unlike the genealogy of Seth in Gen. 5, each entry of the genealogy of Shem does not end with the phrase, "And he died." The line of Seth ended with the Flood and worldwide destruction, but the line of Shem looks forward to Abraham and worldwide blessing.

- *Through the genealogy of Shem, the world-*
- *wide scope of Gen. 1–11 gives way to a partic-*
- *ular family, that of Abraham. But the peoples*
- *of the world are not forgotten. Abraham's call*
- *was for the specific purpose of bringing God's*
- *blessing back to the nations (12:3).*

QUESTIONS TO GUIDE YOUR STUDY

1. What was the problem with the building of the tower of Babel?
2. What is the connection between the tower of Babel and the city of Babylon?
3. What is the purpose of the genealogy of Shem in the story of Genesis?

THE LIFE OF ABRAHAM: FAITH AND OBEDIENCE (GEN. 11:27–25:18)

The primeval history section of the Book of Genesis leaves the reader with the question, How can the relationship between God and mankind which was present in the Garden of Eden be restored? The answer is provided in Gen. 12–50, the patriarchal history section of the book. Here Moses shows that the relationship between God and mankind is restored through the work of God in calling Abraham and his family, and in their response to God through faith and obedience.

As Moses presented the lives of the patriarchs in Genesis, he was careful to portray Abraham as a

The Hebrew word for "name" is *shem*, which is also the name of Noah's son and Abraham's ancestor (10:1). Moses placed the story of the tower of Babel after the table of nations, which ends with the sons of Shem (10:31), and before the genealogy of Shem (11:10) to highlight the attempt of the builders of Babel to build their own "name" (*shem*). In contrast, God, through the line of Shem, would announce to Abraham that "I will make your name (*shem*) great" (12:2).

Seventy names are found in the table of nations. Luke, the only New Testament writer who was a Gentile, was the only Gospel writer to report that Jesus sent seventy disciples into the surrounding towns and villages to announce His coming (Luke 10:1). By thus alluding to the table of nations, Luke indicated the followers of Jesus would reach all the nations of the world. Luke composed a first-century "table of nations" when, in the Book of Acts, he listed the peoples who were present in Jerusalem at Pentecost (Acts 2:9–11).

man who grew in faith and obedience. The readers of Genesis in Moses' day were concerned with meeting God's standards of righteousness. Abraham provided an example for them; he was able to live a righteous life apart from the demands of the Law. He provides the same example for Christians today (Rom. 4:1–2, 13–15).

The Promise (11:27–12:9)

The theme of the patriarchal history section of Genesis is promise. God's fivefold promise to Abram was unconditional and eternal, setting the stage for the formation of a new people, Israel.

The Bridge to Abram (11:27–32)

Genesis 11:27–32 provides a bridge between the primeval history and the patriarchal history sections of Genesis. These verses introduce the major characters who begin the patriarchal history: Abram, his wife Sarai, his brother Nahor, and his nephew Lot. Together these persons, with their father Terah, left Ur of the Chaldees in southern Mesopotamia and settled in Haran, five hundred miles up the Euphrates River.

■ *Of all the people on earth, God chose one,*
■ *Abram, to bring His blessing to the rest.*

The Promise for Abram (12:1–3)

Like the opening scene of Creation (1:3), the story of the patriarchs begins with God speaking. God called Abram to leave his family and homeland and go, childless, to a land that he had never seen (12:1). God then gave Abram a five-fold promise:

1. "I will show you" a land (12:1).

2. "I will make you into a great nation" (12:2).

3. "I will bless you" (12:2).

4. "I will make your name great" (12:2).

5. "You will be a blessing" (12:2).

Each of these promises is grounded in the relationship God established with Adam and Eve in the Garden of Eden and which He desired to maintain with their descendants.

1. The promise of land was intended to provide Abram's descendants a physical homeland where they could live in harmony with God. This promise speaks to everyone's need for security, peace, and "belongingness." It looks forward to God's people participating in the "rest" which He experienced after the Creation (2:2–3).

2. The promise to be a great nation is connected to the "seed" promise of Gen. 3:15. Since the fall of man, God chose certain lines of human descent to carry forward the promise that He would send a deliverer to crush Satan. That line now flowed through Abram to the great nation, Israel, which would descend from him.

3. When God blesses someone, He intervenes in their life to do good things. God blessed Adam and Eve at Creation so they would "be fruitful and multiply" and have dominion over the rest of creation (1:28; cp. 9:1–2). God's blessing to Abram incorporated these elements and caused Abram to prosper in all that he did.

4. To be given a great name is to have a good reputation and a secure identity.

God called Abram, the son of Terah, to a new land (12:1–3). Years later God established His covenant with Abram and changed his name to Abraham (17:1–8). The name Abram means "exalted father," a name which probably refers to the exaltation of Terah's god as the "father" of Abram, in keeping with the practice of naming children in ancient Mesopotamia (cp. Josh. 24:2). The name Abraham is a play on the phrase "father of a multitude" (17:5), indicating God's commitment to fulfilling His promises to Abram. With his name change, Abram's identity was no longer tied to his father's god but to his God-given descendants.

Many scholars date the lives of the patriarchs to some time in the early centuries of the second millennium B.C., around 1800–1600 B.C. The description of the world of the patriarchs portrayed in the Bible best fits what is known about the social, religious, political, and legal world of the ancient Near East from that time. Although the patriarchs are not mentioned in any ancient records other than the Bible, personal names similar to theirs are known.

The builders of the tower of Babel tried to make a name for themselves (11:4) and thereby gain power and prestige before the world and in the face of God. Abram's power and prestige, on the other hand, was to come directly from God.

5. The first four promises lead to the fifth: Abraham was to be a blessing to others. How this would happen is described in Gen. 12:3. God chose the family of Abram through which He would channel His blessings to the nations of the world, thereby drawing all nations to Himself (cp. Gen. 10).

Scholars disagree about the extent to which these promises have been fulfilled. All recognize that Abram received a partial fulfillment of some of the promises during his lifetime: his reputation was enhanced before others, he spent many years in the land of Canaan, and eventually he had a son (Heb. 11:8–19). But what of their final fulfillment?

Some interpreters hold that the promises made to Abram were fulfilled with the kingdoms of David and Solomon—a time when Israel was highly regarded among the nations. Others maintain that they will be literally fulfilled for the Jews only in a still future messianic kingdom. Many find their fulfillment in the Church, since the writers of the New Testament used the promises made to Abram to explain God's relationship to the Church (see Gal. 4:21–31).

Whether these promises find their ultimate fulfillment in the Church, Christians are privileged to receive God's blessings through them (Gal. 3:6–9).

■ *Abraham was chosen by God to be the custo-*
■ *dian of His promises and thereby bring God's*
■ *blessing to all the peoples of the world. These*
■ *promises derive from the blessings that God*
■ *bestowed on Adam and Eve at Creation.*

There is always a temptation to dismiss the stories of the great people of the Bible because their deeds were either too grand, too evil, or too fantastic to be relevant today. In actuality, the men and women of the Bible were real people who faced life with trepidation and, at times, bewilderment. Rarely were their deeds wholly good or wholly evil. Those such as Abraham whom we are called to emulate were people of faith, but, like us, they sometimes disbelieved. By their example and God's power, we can learn to walk with God.

The Response of Abram (12:4–9)

Abram obeyed the call of God even though he was entering the great unknown (12:4). Abram, Sarai, and Lot crossed the land of Canaan from north to south, stopping to build altars at Shechem and on a mountain east of Bethel (12:6–8).

This episode emphasizes Abram's initial obedience, yet foreshadows future trouble. At Shechem God told Abram, "I will give this land to your descendants" (12:7, NCV), but the Canaanites already lived there (12:6). Abram continued traveling toward the south (12:9).

The tension introduced by these verses continues throughout not only Genesis but the entire Old Testament. How are the people of God to live in light of the promises of God when the promises are not yet fulfilled? The story of the patriarchs is very much the story of God's promises constantly being put in jeopardy by the circumstances of life.

These circumstances were often the actions or inactions, the obstinacy or sheer inability of Abraham and his family to live in accordance with God's promises. In the meantime, God worked calmly and purposefully to establish His promises by repeating them to Abraham, Isaac, and Jacob.

- Like us, Abraham had to grow in faith and
- obedience. His initial response to God was to
- obey. Future circumstances would cause Abra-
- ham sometimes to doubt, sometimes to believe.

Living a Life of Promise in a Hostile World, Part I (12:10–14:24)

The next three stories focus on the connection between the promise of land (12:1) and the nations that surrounded that land.

The Promise Threatened in Egypt (12:10–20)

It is not known how long Abram was in his land of promise before a famine struck and he was forced to go to Egypt. From the way the story is told, Abram left quickly and willingly (12:10). In Egypt, Abram passed the beautiful Sarai off as his sister lest the Egyptians kill him to marry her; Pharaoh promptly took her into his harem (12:11–15).

Abram was in the southern part of Canaan (NIV "Negev") when a severe famine struck the land. The Negev is an area of marginal rainfall highly susceptible to famine. Egypt, by contrast, was the breadbasket of the eastern Mediterranean world in ancient times. Although it receives virtually no rainfall, Egypt's fertile lands are watered by the Nile River.

Within a few short verses of his divine call, Abram had given up his land, his wife and, with her, all hope for a son. But God intervened on Abram's behalf. Pharaoh recognized God's hand in his affliction and sent Abram and Sarai back to Canaan (12:19–20). The pattern for the patriarchal history is thus set: God sees to it that His purposes are accomplished in spite of the actions of others (cp. 50:20). Through it all, He moves to increase faith and obedience in His people.

- Abraham at first behaved as if he were
- unsure of the ramifications of God's prom-
- ises. God's intervention through Pharaoh put
- him back on track.

The Separation of Abram and Lot (13:1–18)
Back in Canaan, the herdsmen of Abram and
Lot fought over access to the limited water
resources in the land (13:2–7). Abram, wishing
to maintain peace within his family, suggested
that Lot move wherever he would like. Lot
promptly chose the well-watered Jordan River
valley to the east (13:8–11).

The area of Lot's choice was already home to the
prosperous yet decadent cities of Sodom and
Gomorrah, cities that God would later destroy
(19:24–28). Lot moved his tent close to Sodom,
where the men "were wicked and were sinning
greatly against the LORD" (13:13).

As in the story of Cain and Abel, struggle was
followed by separation. By moving east, both
Cain (4:16) and Lot (13:11) left their
God-chosen families. Abram stayed where he
belonged, in the land of promise, where God
again promised him the land and many descendants (13:14–15).

Genesis 13 ends with a note that Abraham
finally settled by the oak trees of Mamre, east of
Hebron (13:18), in the southern part of the
Canaanite hill country. The region of Hebron
became a home base for Abraham (18:1), eventually serving as his burial ground (25:9).

The land promised
to Abram had stony
ground and scarce
water resources.
Much of it was
rugged. It was a hard
land from which to
scratch out a living.
Daily survival was
much easier in
Mesopotamia and
Egypt, where the
wealth of the world
was concentrated on
broad, well-watered
plains (cp. 13:10).
God chose a difficult
land as the home for
His people to teach
them they had to
depend on Him for
survival—not their
own efforts or what
the world had to offer
(Deut. 11:10–12).

Ancient records from Mesopotamia dating to the time of Abram suggest that no single Mesopotamian king was strong enough to fight a strong enemy without forming a coalition with other kings. None of the Mesopotamian kings mentioned in Gen. 14:1 has been positively identified with any known historical figure. Some scholars have suggested that Amraphel, king of Shinar, was the well-known Babylonian king Hammurabi, but this is doubtful.

■ *Lot left the land of promise and placed him-*
■ *self in a position where he would be influ-*
■ *enced by the sinful behavior of others.*
■ *Abraham stayed where God wanted him and*
■ *again received the promise of God's blessing.*

Abram's Victory and Melchizedek's Blessing (14:1–24)

Genesis 14 opens with an account of war between two coalitions of kings. The kings of five cities located somewhere near the Salt Sea (14:3; the Dead Sea), including Sodom and Gomorrah, had been vassals of four kings from Mesopotamia (14:1–4). When they rebelled, the Mesopotamian kings marched to the Dead Sea, overrunning everyone in their path (14:5–7). The kings from the Dead Sea were defeated, their wealth was plundered, and Lot was taken captive (14:11–12).

When Abram was told of Lot's capture, he responded with force. Abram and his men overtook and defeated the Mesopotamian kings, rescuing Lot in the process (14:13–16). In Gen. 19 Lot would again need to be rescued, this time from Sodom.

Psalm 110, a messianic psalm, speaks of an individual who is both a mighty king from Zion and an eternal priest "in the order of Melchizedek" (Ps. 110:2–4). The writer of the Book of Hebrews declared this individual to be Jesus (Heb. 7) and explained how Melchizedek was a type (or picture) of Jesus.

Upon returning home, Abram was met by both the king of Sodom and Melchizedek, king of Salem (Jerusalem). Melchizedek, who was also "priest of God Most High," blessed both Abram and God (14:18–20). Abram responded by giving Melchizedek a tithe, thus recognizing the validity of his priesthood. Not to be outdone, the king of Sodom offered to let Abram keep the booty that he had recovered, but Abram refused (14:21–24).

N

- Abram showed himself to be a man of integ-
- rity. He was loyal to his nephew Lot; yet, he
- was not about to make a deal with Lot's col-
- league from Sodom. By accepting the bless-
- ing of Melchizedek, Abram elevated God in
- the eyes of two Canaanite kings.

The Covenant Relationship (15:1–18:15)

Chapters 15 through 18 of Genesis form a repeating pattern based on content. Genesis 15 and 17 report two encounters between Abraham and God in which a covenant relationship was formally established between the two, ratifying the promise of Gen. 12:2 that Abraham would be the father of a great nation. Each of these chapters is followed by a tender glimpse at the private lives of Abraham and Sarah and the difficulties they faced in having a family.

The Covenant Established (15:1–21)

The lack of a son must have weighed heavily on Abram, an aging man in a patriarchal society. According to custom, he had named one of his servants, Eliezer of Damascus, as heir (15:2–3). In the first recorded conversation between Abram and God, God came to Abram in a vision and told him that He Himself was Abram's reward (15:1). Abram's heart, however, was with the son he didn't have: "What can you give me since I remain childless?" (15:2).

God's reply was to show Abram the night sky and tell him that his own descendants would number no less than the stars (15:5). Abram "believed the LORD," and God counted his belief as righteousness (15:6).

The story of Abram in Gen. 14 provides an example of "being in the world but not of it" (cp. John 17:18; Rom. 12:2). The people of Sodom, a corrupt city, had a physical need and Abram came to their aid. Clearly he was not isolated from society. On the other hand, by turning down payment from the king of Sodom, Abram refused to be identified with negative aspects of society. Abram's response showed that he was to be involved with affairs of the world but only in ways that were consistent with God's blessing (Stuart Briscoe, *Mastering the Old Testament*, vol. 1, *Genesis*, [Word Publishing, 1987], pp. 138–39).

God judged Abram's righteousness not according to a written standard of laws (which Abram didn't have) but according to proper conduct in his relationship with Him. This distinction was vitally important for the Israelites of Moses' day—persons who had received God's laws at Mt. Sinai (Exod. 20). For Moses, Abram provided an example that the proper object of belief is God—not His Law—and that faith in God is necessary for obedience.

After Abram believed, God confirmed His promise to give Abram the land in which he was living. That confirmation involved a bizarre ceremony in which a smoking fire pot and a flaming torch, two objects which represented God, passed between the severed body parts of sacrificed animals (15:9–11, 17; cp. Jer. 34:17–20). God revealed that Abram's descendants would be slaves in Egypt for four hundred years but then would return to Canaan (15:13–21). Clearly Abram's life was part of a divine plan.

The word *covenant* first appears in the story of Abram in Gen. 15:18. God formally entered into a covenant relationship with Abram only after he was declared righteous because of his faith (15:6). The covenant with Abram was unconditional and exclusive. Abram was not required to do anything to receive either the land or descendants, but he *was* expected to believe in God alone. God, on the other hand, obligated Himself by the terms of the covenant to act on Abram's behalf.

■ *Abram's faith in God in spite of difficult circumstances provided the flagship example of faith for later biblical writers. God's cove-*

■ nant with Abram was a formal means of rec-
■ ognizing that He would bless His people.

The Birth of Ishmael (16:1–16)

Having entered into a covenant relationship
with God, Abram tried through his own effort to
fulfill God's obligation to provide a son. God
had rejected Abram's choice of a man from
Damascus to be his heir (15:2–4). At the
prompting of Sarai, Abram had a child with her
maid, Hagar, a woman from Egypt (16:1–4).

Abram assumed that Hagar's child, considered
his heir according to the prevailing custom of
the day, would be acceptable to God (cp.
17:18). Not only did Abram not continue to
wait for his own son; he sought an heir from a
nation which stood outside of God's promise
(cp. Deut. 7:1–6).

When Hagar became pregnant, she began to
taunt and mock Sarai (16:4), who responded by
treating Hagar so harshly that she fled into the
wilderness (16:6). The angel of the LORD found
Hagar and told her to return home where she
would have a son, Ishmael. Ishmael would grow
into a wild man and live at odds with his brothers (16:7–12).

The implication is clear: Ishmael was blessed,
but the mighty nation that would come from
him would not be Abram's promised heir.

In the Old
Testament, the term
Ishmaelites generally
refers to any number
of desert tribes living
on the outskirts of the
land of Israel (cp.
25:12–18). The
caravan of traders
which took Joseph to
Egypt consisted of
Ishmaelites and
Midianites (37:25–28;
the Midianites were a
large tribe whose
home stretched from
Sinai to Arabia). In the
days of Gideon, the
Ishmaelites, the
Midianites, and
"people of the east"
oppressed Israel
(Judg. 8:22–24; cp.
Judg. 6:3). Today the
Ishmaelites are
usually identified with
the Arabs.

■ Impatience, one-upmanship, jealousy—
■ Abram, Hagar, and Sarai each exhibited these
■ traits; yet, their actions can be understood in
■ the light of typical family relationships
■ and how they work. Moses clearly showed
■ through these narratives that actions have

Circumcision, which was widespread in ancient times, is known from Asia, Africa, Australia, and the Americas but not Europe. Among Israel's neighbors, circumcision was practiced in Egypt and Canaan but not Assyria, Babylonia, or Philistia (cp. 1 Sam. 17:26; 2 Sam. 1:20). Circumcision was—and still is—practiced generally for physical (medicinal or hygienic), social, or religious reasons. Most cultures circumcise male infants as a rite of puberty. Genesis 17 describes the unique significance which circumcision was given in ancient Israel.

- *consequences. The divine call of Abram,*
- *although certain and irrevocable, had to be*
- *worked out among the foibles of human beings.*

The Covenant Reestablished (17:1–27)

Genesis 17 brings issues relating to the promise of an heir for Abraham to a critical point. Abram was now ninety-nine and Sarai only ten years younger. Thirteen years had passed since the birth of Ishmael, and Abram knew it was physically impossible for him and Sarai to have a child on their own (17:17).

Nevertheless, God renewed his covenant with Abram. This covenant was a formal agreement between God, the superior party, and Abram, his subject. God introduced Himself with the words, "I am God Almighty" (*El Shaddai;* 17:1). By this title, He declared His all-sufficient power and might, and thereby His right to dictate the terms of the covenant to Abram.

God correlated the covenant with righteousness. After introducing Himself, God commanded, "Walk before me and be blameless" (17:1). The covenant would become the vehicle through which Abram and his descendants could live rightly, patterning their lives after Enoch (5:24) and Noah (6:9), earlier personalities who had "walked with God."

As part of the covenant agreement, God promised to give Abram a multitude of descendants (17:2–6). God changed Abram's name, which means "exalted father," to Abraham, "father of a multitude," as a perpetual reminder of this promise. God also promised to establish His covenant with Abraham's descendants, granting them the land of Canaan as an everlasting possession (17:7–8).

God then changed Sarai's name to Sarah, "princess," promising that she would bear a son within a year. While Ishmael would become a great nation, Sarah's own son Isaac would receive God's covenant (17:20–21).

Unlike the terms of the covenant which God had established with Abram in Gen. 15, the renewed covenant in Gen. 17 required that all males who wanted to participate be circumcised (17:10–14). The physical act of circumcision was both a sign that the covenant was in place and a seal binding the parties of the covenant together.

The act of circumcision involved both obligation and participation in a common heritage. Abraham and his descendants were obligated to live according to God's covenant. Because the covenant was first established in the context of Abram's faith (15:6, 18), the Israelites were also obligated to enter into the covenant by faith. Because Abraham served only God, the Israelites were obligated to serve only God.

God was obligated to fulfill the divine promises that He had first spoken to Abram in Haran (12:1–3). These promises formed a common heritage for those who entered into the covenant.

As the writer of Genesis and the other books of the Pentateuch, Moses recognized that circumcision was an outward sign pointing to an inward heart attitude (Deut. 10:16). Nevertheless, during the time of the New Testament, some Jewish Christians insisted that non-Jewish converts be circumcised in order to participate in the blessings of Abraham's covenant (Acts 15:1).

The apostle Paul countered that circumcision was of no importance in the eyes of God, who accepted Jews and Gentiles alike if they obeyed Him (1 Cor. 7:19; cp. Gal. 3:28; Col. 2:11).

■ *The covenant between God and Abraham*
■ *was a basic element in God's redemptive plan*
■ *for mankind. Abraham's obligation to obey*
■ *and God's obligation to bless established the*
■ *pattern for a formal relationship between*
■ *God and His people.*

The Birth of Isaac Announced (18:1–15)

Three visitors—really the LORD (18:1, 10)—came to Abraham's tent and informed him that the next spring Sarah would conceive a son (18:10). Sarah, who was listening to their conversation, laughed to herself, as would be expected for a woman well past childbearing age (18:11–12). God knew that she laughed, and He asked, "Is anything too hard (literally, "too wonderful" or "too extraordinary") for the LORD?" (18:14).

Sarah did not believe God's promise (18:15). This was an understandable response, given her circumstances. There is no indication in Genesis that Sarah was present when Abraham had his previous covenantal encounters with God (chaps. 15 and 17). The divine announcement in Gen. 18 left Sarah in suspense, wondering how God would do the impossible.

■ *God's promise that Abraham and Sarah*
■ *would have a son now had a specific timeta-*
■ *ble. From a human perspective, God had*
■ *waited too long; but God's sovereign plan*
■ *was right on track.*

Living a Life of Promise in a Hostile World, Part II (18:16–20:18)

The story of the birth of a child to Abraham and Sarah is interrupted by three episodes that again drew Abraham into the larger world scene. Abraham's involvement with Sodom and Gomorrah showed him to be a man of faith; yet, his interaction with the king of Gerar raised troubling questions.

Abraham's Bargain (18:16–33)

God revealed to Abraham His plan to rescue Lot and his family from Sodom's imminent destruction (18:17–21; cp. 19:12–13). The reason God gave for allowing Abraham to be "in the know" is striking: Abraham was chosen by God to instruct his children in the ways of the LORD so God's promise to bless the world would be fulfilled through them (18:19; cp. 12:3).

Abraham accepted his responsibility as trustee of the divine promises by bargaining with God over the destruction of Sodom (18:22–33). How much righteousness was necessary to prevent evil from being destroyed? Is justice served through the destruction of innocent people?

After several passionate pleas by Abraham, God agreed that if there were only ten righteous people in Sodom, the entire city would be spared. God then left to do what was right while Abraham returned home, convinced that God would do what was just (18:25, 33).

Moses portrayed Abraham as a type of himself, one who would intercede boldly before God on behalf of an erring people (cp. Exod. 32:11–14). When Moses interceded for Israel, he did so on the basis of the patriarchal promises (Exod. 32:13).

- *Abraham was willing to intercede before God*
- *on behalf of others. While God is forgiving, He*
- *does not tolerate flagrant disobedience.*

The Destruction of Sodom and Gomorrah (19:1–38)

The stories of the covenant relationship (15:1–18:15) are framed by two stories of Sodom and Lot (14:1–24; 18:16–19:29). Together, these stories show the effects of sin on a person who places himself outside the covenant blessings of God.

The story of the destruction of Sodom and Gomorrah portrays sin at its worst. The contrast

Scholars disagree about the location of the "cities of the plain" (Sodom, Gomorrah, Admah, Zeboiim, and Zoar), the five cities of Gen. 14:2–3 which—it is assumed—were destroyed by God (Gen. 19:24–28). Some locate the cities at the northern end of the Dead Sea; others place them at the southern end. Archaeological evidence is largely lacking. The remains of five ancient cities lying east of the Dead Sea are often appealed to as the ruins of the "cities of the plain," but they were destroyed centuries before Abraham's time.

The destruction of Sodom because of its extreme wickedness became a point of comparison for later biblical writers. With blistering words, the prophets compared the sin of Israel to that of Sodom (Isa. 1:10; 3:9; Jer. 23:14; Amos 4:11; Zeph. 2:9). Jesus used the example of Sodom to castigate those who did not believe Him (Matt. 10:15; 11:23–24; Luke 10:12; 17:28–30).

between the intense concern for others shown by Abraham (Gen. 18) and the flagrant disregard for human decency by the men of Sodom (Gen. 19) is so striking that it is grotesque. The narrative of Gen. 19 is brilliantly written to tell a horrifying story.

The visitors (now called "angels" by Moses lest we miss the point) entered the house of Lot and were immediately surrounded by all the men of Sodom intent on homosexual rape (19:3–10). After striking the mob with blindness (19:11), Lot's guests announced the city's impending doom and warned Lot and his family to flee (19:12–13). Lot, his wife, and two daughters fled, but hesitantly and only to a nearby town that they had convinced the men not to destroy (19:15–23).

God then destroyed Sodom and Gomorrah by fire and brimstone (19:24–29). Lot was saved in spite of himself. This was a clear testimony of the divine blessing bestowed on Abraham (12:2).

After Sodom was destroyed, Lot's daughters impregnated themselves by their father who lay drunk in his tent (19:30–38). Each bore a son, Moab and Ammon, the ancestors of two nations that would become enemies of Israel—once Israel settled in the land of Canaan. This episode is reminiscent of the drunkenness of Noah (9:20–27), reinforcing the necessity to participate in a covenant relationship with God.

■ *God destroyed Sodom and Gomorrah, bastions of sinful behavior, but mercifully provided a way for Lot to escape if he chose to*

- *believe God's word of warning. Lot was*
- *saved because he believed, although his own*
- *family proved unfaithful.*

The Promise Threatened in Gerar (20:1–18)

The last episode before the birth of Isaac, who was the long-awaited fulfillment of the promise, parallels the first episode to take place after the promise had been given. Abraham had passed off his wife as his sister while in Egypt to save his own life (12:10–20). Now in Gerar, a city within the land promised to Abraham, he did the same thing, defending his integrity to the king Abimelech: "She really is my sister, the daughter of my father though not of my mother" (20:12).

Abraham's reason for acting again as he had in Egypt had not changed in spite of his subsequent encounters with God (15:1–20; 17:1–18:15). Even though Abraham knew that his promised son was to be born by Sarah, he still was willing to give her up to save his own life.

After all, reasoned Abraham, "There is surely no fear of God in this place" (20:11). Living too close to the men of Sodom had blinded the eyes of his nephew Lot to the things of God. Living too close to Gerar now blinded Abraham's heart to the power of God. His old ways of thinking were not yet totally subdued.

In telling this story of Abraham, Moses went to great lengths to explain both Abimelech's innocence and his openness to the things of God (20:3–8). Abimelech lectured Abraham on righteous behavior much as a father would correct his naive but errant son (20:9–10). Abimelech opened his land and wealth to Abraham in deference to his status as a prophet of God (cp. 20:7).

"It is possible to miscalculate in many areas of life but there is no greater miscalculation than the one that assumes either that God is disinterested in human affairs or is incapable of intervention. . . Abraham's carefully laid plans had run into the roadblock of divine control for which he would eventually be immensely grateful" (Stuart Briscoe, *Mastering the Old Testament, vol. 1, Genesis,* [Word Publishing, 1987], pp. 138–39).

In bold contrast to the men of Sodom, the actions of Abimelech are clear evidence that people who stand outside of a formal covenant relationship with God can respond favorably to Him. And in spite of Abraham's lapse of righteous behavior, God still blessed him (20:16–17).

- Although old habits die hard, God rescued
- Abraham from the consequences of his
- behavior. Abraham was not always faithful
- to the terms of the covenant, but God was.

The Promise Fulfilled (21:1–25:18)

The story of the life of Abraham ends with events surrounding the birth and early years of Isaac, the son of Abraham and Sarah.

The Birth of Isaac (21:1–21)

Isaac is a play on a Hebrew word which means "to laugh."

Sarah gave birth to a son just as God had said (21:1–3; cp. 17:16; 18:10). She named him Isaac. Sarah's sense of humor, which had been tried during her long wait for a son, at last found joyful release (18:12–15; 21:6–7). Isaac was circumcised to confirm that he had been born under the covenant (21:4; cp. 17:10–13).

Sarah's laughter stopped cold when she saw Ishmael, the no-longer heir apparent, playing with Isaac (21:9). For Sarah there was no longer any reason to tolerate either Ishmael or his mother Hagar since both kept alive memories of her own barrenness and Hagar's previous scorn (16:4–5). Sarah banished Ishmael and Hagar—this time for good (cp. 16:6–9)—lest Isaac have to share his rightful inheritance (21:10).

Because Ishmael was Abraham's son, God provided for him and his mother as they forged a new life in the wilderness of Paran (21:11–21). Ishmael received God's blessing—like Isaac, he would father a great nation—but he stood outside the covenant relationship with God (21:13, 18; cp. 16:10).

■ With the birth of Isaac, the promise of an
■ heir—a promise that God had uttered as
■ early as Gen. 3:15—received its first fulfill-
■ ment. Through him, God's covenant of prom-
■ ise could continue.

The Covenant between Abraham and Abimelech (21:22–34)

Abimelech, king of Gerar (cp. 20:1–18), recognized that God was with Abraham, so he entered into a covenant relationship with him at Beer-sheba (21:23–30). This covenant, based on mutual loyalty and trust, allowed Abraham and Abimelech—and their herdsmen—to live in peace with one another.

The covenant relationship between Abraham and Abimelech was a down payment on the promise of God to bless the nations through Abraham (12:3).

■ The relationship of Abraham and Abimelech
■ represents the type of relationship that God
■ intended Israel to have with all its neigh-
■ bors—an ideal seldom met in later Israelite
■ history.

The location of the "land of Moriah" is uncertain. Clues in Genesis place it a three-day journey from Beer-sheba (21:33–34; 22:4), but the direction Abraham traveled is not known. Later Jewish tradition identified the place with the hill on which the temple in Jerusalem was built—a hill called Mt. Moriah in 2 Chron. 3:1. This tradition was accepted by the Muslims, who also believe that the son of Abraham in this case was not Isaac but Ishmael. The Samaritans believe that the land of Moriah was in the vicinity of Shechem, their sacred city.

The Obedience of Abraham (22:1–24)

Christians sometimes refer to the story recorded in Gen. 22 as "the sacrifice of Isaac." Jews call it "the binding of Isaac"—a better title since Isaac was bound but not sacrificed (22:9). The focus of the story is not on the destiny of Isaac but the obedience of Abraham.

Just when the promises of God were beginning to be fulfilled, Abraham faced the greatest challenge of his life. In tender yet unmistakably clear words, God commanded Abraham to give his long-awaited son back to Him as a burnt offering: "Take your son, your only son, Isaac, whom you love . . ." (22:2). This horribly incomprehensible deed was to take place in the land of Moriah.

In commanding Abraham to go to Moriah, God used the same Hebrew words (literally, "Get yourself gone") which he had first used to call Abraham into Canaan years before (22:2; cp. 12:1). In the mind of Abraham, God's promise was to end on the same note with which it had been given. The first command involved hope and life; the second contained despair and death.

Abraham dutifully went to Mt. Moriah, believing that God would provide whatever was necessary for a proper burnt offering (22:3–8). Just before Abraham drove his knife into his son, God stayed his hand and commanded him to offer instead a ram caught in a nearby thicket (22:9–14).

Moses called God's command a "test" (22:1), indicating that God didn't necessarily want Isaac killed. In fact, God wanted to determine if Abraham was trusting *Him*, or just His promises. Abraham did not know that he was being tested (the most effective test is the one which we do not know is happening) and did what God told him to do. By obeying God without question or hesitation, Abraham's faith was proven to be sound (Heb. 11:17–19; James 2:21–22).

Abraham passed the test and was found to be a trustworthy repository of God's promises. God responded to Abraham's acts of faith by reaffirming His promises in the strongest terms yet given: "I will *surely* bless you . . . because you have obeyed me" (22:17). For the original audience of Genesis—a people who had witnessed the revelation of God's requirements at Mt. Sinai—Moses had forged a connection between faith and obedience.

■ *By obeying God without question in the*
■ *hardest test of his life, Abraham proved he*
■ *was a man of faith. By allowing Isaac to live,*
■ *God showed He was true to His promises.*

The Death of Sarah (23:1–20)

With the promise of a son secure in the person of Isaac, Sarah's role was fulfilled. Genesis 23 records her death (23:1–2) and the preparations which Abraham made for her burial. In his deep grief, Abraham bought a plot of land with a burial cave in Machpelah, east of Hebron, from Ephron the Hittite (23:3–20).

Abraham's negotiations with the Hittites of Hebron are a picture of dignity and respect. Abraham claimed to be "an alien and a stranger" in the land (23:4), but the Hittites called him a "mighty prince among us" (23:6). The Hittites offered Abraham use of their burial caves at no

The near-sacrifice of Isaac in Gen. 22 has messianic significance in two ways. Like Isaac, Jesus was a "seed" of Abraham who silently submitted Himself to being sacrificed. Also like Isaac (Gen. 22:6), Jesus (John 19:17) carried the wood on which He was to die. But like the ram, Jesus was a substitute who, through His sacrifice, gave life to others. Because of the work of Jesus, Christians can, like Isaac, be living sacrifices (Rom. 12:1).

The Hittites were a large and influential group in the second millennium B.C. Their homeland was on the Anatolian plateau (modern central Turkey). Ancient records note individual Hittites living in various lands along the eastern Mediterranean shoreline. Archaeologists have uncovered evidence of Hittite cultural influence in Canaan. Hebron, an important city in the hill country of southern Canaan, was evidently a Hittite enclave.

cost, but Abraham wanted to establish formal property rights in the land (23:8–16).

The burial cave at Machpelah became Abraham's down payment on the land of promise. It served as the burial place for him (25:9) and several of his descendants: Isaac (35:29), Rebekah (49:29–31), Leah (49:31), and Jacob (50:13).

■ *The patriarchs never owned the land promised*
■ *them, but they lay there in death. Their claim*
■ *on the land secured the right of Moses and*
■ *Joshua to bring the Israelites back to Canaan.*

A Wife for Isaac (24:1–67)

Genesis 24 is a sensitive account of loyalty, divine guidance, hospitality, and love. Conforming to the custom of arranged marriages, Abraham sent his servant (perhaps Eliezer; 24:2; cp. 15:2–3) back to his homeland in Haran to select and bring back a wife for Isaac.

Isaac was not to take a wife from among the Canaanites, for they stood outside the line of God's covenant blessing (24:3; cp. 9:25–26). Abraham instructed his servant in the urgency of the matter by reciting to him the covenant promises and having him take an oath (24:2–9). As part of the oath, the servant touched Abraham "under the thigh" (at the point of circumcision, the sign of the covenant; 24:2, 9; cp. 47:29) in order to seal the seriousness of the upcoming venture.

Upon arriving in Haran, Abraham's servant, with the help of God, chose Rebekah, the granddaughter of Abraham's brother, as a wife for Isaac (24:10–27). Rebekah was a woman of

"We can all see God in exceptional things, but it requires the growth of spiritual discipline to see God in every detail. Never believe that the so-called random events of life are anything less than God's appointed order. Be ready to discover His divine designs anywhere and everywhere" (Oswald Chambers, *My Utmost for His Highest,* [Oswald Chambers Publications Association Ltd., 1992], November 14).

great charm and energy, essential qualities for a difficult life in Canaan.

Rebekah's family had known about God since the call of Abraham years before (11:31–12:3). Now Abraham's servant told them of how God had blessed Abraham (24:34–49). Rebekah's father, Bethuel, and her brother, Laban, let Rebekah return with Abraham's servant, acknowledging that "this is from the LORD" (24:50). Rebekah went willingly (24:56–61), and Isaac loved and married her (24:67).

- *The marriage of Isaac and Rebekah was*
- *arranged by both Abraham and God; yet, it*
- *was a marriage of love.*

The Death and Legacy of Abraham (25:1–18)

Just before recording the death of Abraham, Moses noted that Abraham married for a second time (25:1). With his new wife Keturah, Abraham had six additional sons (25:2). The names of several of these sons and their descendants (25:3–4) correspond to the names of desert tribes living south and east of Canaan. These children, like Ishmael, participated in the blessing of God through Abraham but stood outside of God's covenant (25:6; cp. 16:10; 21:18).

Abraham died at the age of 175 and was buried next to Sarah in the cave of Machpelah that he had purchased at Hebron (25:7–10; cp. 23:19). Abraham did not inherit the land, but his bones rested there (cp. Heb. 11:8–16). Isaac and Ishmael buried Abraham.

Although Isaac was younger than Ishmael, he is mentioned first. This is a clear indication that at

Abraham's servant, after traveling a long distance, met Rebekah, Isaac's future wife, at a well. Both Jacob (Gen. 29:1–12) and Moses (Exod. 2:15–22) also found their future wives at a well after long journeys.

These stories anticipate an event in the life of Jesus reported in John 4. On His long walk home from Jerusalem, Jesus stopped at a well in Sychar, where He also met a woman, although of rather different reputation (John 4:1–26). This woman had been married to several different husbands. As a result of Jesus' visit, the entire town believed in Him and participated in the promises of God (John 4:39–42).

the death of Abraham, the role of custodian of the covenant promises had passed to him. God blessed Isaac after his father's death (25:11).

The account of the life of Abraham ends with the genealogy of Ishmael. Ishmael had twelve sons (25:12–15) who became "tribal rulers" (25:16) and lived "in hostility toward all their brothers" in the vast desert lands south and east of Canaan (25:18).

The mention of twelve tribal rulers in connection with Ishmael is intended to set the Ishmaelites apart as a new and distinct people, parallel to the twelve tribes of Israel in structure but alienated from their covenant relationship with God.

■ *By the time Abraham died, he was the father*
■ *of not one nation but many; and these nations*
■ *were already being blessed because of him.*

QUESTIONS TO GUIDE YOUR STUDY

1. How were God's promises to Abraham threatened during the life of Abraham? What did God do about it?
2. How does the life of Abraham illustrate the relationship between faith and obedience?
3. How did Abraham become the father of many nations?

THE LIFE OF ISAAC: LINKING ABRAHAM TO ISRAEL (25:19–28:9)

The story of Isaac is told within the context of the lives of Abraham and Jacob. Throughout Genesis, Isaac moves under the shadow of his illustrious father and his strong-willed son. Except for a single wide-eyed question, Isaac was silent as Abraham led him to be bound and sacrificed (22:1–14). Isaac played no role in the choice of Rebekah as his wife (24:1–27).

As head of his own family, Isaac was never quite in charge of affairs, being twice duped by his son Jacob (25:29–34; 27:1–40). In spite of his legal rights, Isaac did all he could to avoid confrontation with the king of Gerar (26:17–33).

What should we make of Isaac? Was he a man of peace and quiet faith or a person who just moved through life, letting things happen to him? Clearly Isaac's personality was very different from the lives of Abraham and Jacob. Yet, Isaac was still blessed by God and became an effective tool in His hands. Isaac transferred God's covenant promises to Jacob, whose twelve children became the twelve tribes of Israel.

The Early Years of Isaac's Sons (25:19–34)

The story of the family of Isaac opens with the birth of Isaac's twin sons, Jacob and Esau. The stage was set for a struggle between these sons which continues to the present time.

The Birth of Jacob and Esau (25:19–26)

Like Sarah, Rebekah was barren and could give birth only through the direct intervention of God (25:20–21). She stands in a long line of people chosen by God who were incapable of fulfilling His promises on their own.

Rebekah conceived twin boys. While in the womb, the babies "jostled" (literally, "crushed") each other (25:22)—a sure indication of their struggles to come. God revealed to Rebekah that her younger son would dominate his older brother and that the two nations that descended from them would be aligned against each other (25:23).

Edom, the name of the nation which descended from Esau, is a play on the word "red," the baby's color at birth (25:25, 30).

Rebekah named her older son Esau. She named her second son Jacob, a play on the word "heel" (25:26). As Jacob grabbed Esau's heel at birth, so he would try to grasp and confound Esau throughout life.

- *The birth of Jacob and Esau anticipated the*
- *ongoing struggle of their lives and the future*
- *of Israel and Edom, the nations that would*
- *descend from them.*

The Stolen Birthright (25:27–34)

The differences between Isaac and Rebekah—country boy and sophisticated city girl—were played out in their children. Isaac favored the out-of-doors son Esau, while Rebekah coddled Jacob (25:27–28).

Jacob, always seeking the upper hand over his brother, took advantage of Esau's famished condition and traded a bowl of stew for Esau's birthright as the elder son (25:29–34). This story is told in such a way that it reveals Esau's character as impulsive, coarse, and uncaring—hardly the type of person suitable for the covenant promises.

Esau's request, "Let me eat," contains a Hebrew verb which normally describes the feeding habits of cattle. Although lentil stew was a well-known staple, Esau called it literally "this red stuff"—hardly something that a sensitive adult would say. After securing the stew, Esau ate and went on his way with no remorse.

Jacob, on the other hand, is presented as cunning and farsighted. The Hebrew verbs used by Jacob indicate that he spoke as a superior to an

The Hebrew word *heel* from which Jacob got his name is related to the verb "to follow at the heel" and hence "to supplant," "to trick," or "to deceive." In describing the character of Israel, Jacob's descendants, the prophet Jeremiah lamented, "The heart is deceitful above all things and beyond cure. Who can understand it?" (Jer. 17:9). The word *deceitful* in this verse is the verb related to the word *heel*. In effect, Jeremiah said, "The heart of everyone is Jacob-like and in desperate need of God."

inferior. Jacob made his stipulations in legal terms, covering himself lest Esau later regret his hasty actions. While the transaction was a legal sale, the relative value of the goods exchanged indicates that Jacob "got a steal."

The story of the stolen birthright, like many of the events of Jacob's life, is theologically complex. Jacob did not act with integrity; yet, God chose to work through him anyway. We can assume that the sovereignty of God, so well established in Genesis, would have provided everything Jacob needed to receive and to pass on the covenant promises. If Jacob needed the birthright and Isaac's blessing to be the chosen heir—and he evidently did—God would have secured those for him without his conniving tricks.

The apostle Paul used the birth of Jacob and Esau to explain God's election of Israel as His chosen people. Paul noted that God chose Jacob over Esau while they were still in the womb (Rom. 9:10–13). Paul then quoted God's statement in Mal. 1:2–3 that He loved Jacob but hated Esau. The doctrine of election, while shrouded in the mystery of God, places God's sovereignty over His creation.

- *Jacob's scheme to secure the birthright that*
- *legally belonged to Esau succeeded, but it left*
- *Esau bitter. Jacob was used by God in spite of*
- *himself.*

Living a Life of Promise in a Hostile World, Part III (26:1–35)

Moses interrupted Jacob's attempt to secure the birthright and blessing by two episodes that portray Isaac as a man of God's promise. Both parallel events that had happened to Abraham.

The Promise Threatened in Gerar (26:1–11)

Isaac, like Abraham, faced a famine (26:1). God told Isaac to remain in the land of Canaan and not go to Egypt as his father had done in similar circumstances (26:2; cp. 12:10). God then reaffirmed the covenant promises to Isaac with much the same language he had used with

In ancient Near Eastern society, the birthright was the legal right of inheritance which belonged to the firstborn son. For a son to hold the birthright meant that he became the head of his extended family at the death of his father. Hence, the patriarchal line continued through him. The birthright also included a double portion of his father's estate—resources which the holder of the birthright would need to provide for the widows and children under his care.

Abraham (26:3–4; cp. 12:1–3; 13:14–17; 15:18–21; 17:6–8, 16; 22:17–18). This God did, not because Isaac deserved it, but because of the prior obedience or faithfulness of Abraham (26:5).

Once in Gerar, Isaac fell into the same trap which had twice ensnared his father (cp. 12:10–20; 20:1–18). Isaac told the people of Gerar that Rebekah was his sister for fear that one of them would kill him in order to take her as his wife (26:6–7).

When King Abimelech (probably the same Abimelech who had experienced similar dealings with Abraham) realized what was happening (again!), he reprimanded Isaac as he had Abraham and then placed him under royal protection (26:8–11). Abimelech again proved himself to be a man of integrity worthy of being blessed by God.

■ *By passing off his wife as his sister, Isaac*
■ *showed that human behavior remains essen-*
■ *tially unchanged from generation to genera-*
■ *tion. By rescuing Isaac, God showed that His*
■ *grace also remains unchanged.*

The Prosperity of Isaac (26:12–35)
God blessed Isaac, and he became so wealthy that the Philistines envied him (26:12–14). Rather than let these ill feelings escalate into open confrontation, Abimelech sent Isaac away (26:16).

Isaac moved, but his herdsmen squabbled with the herdsmen of Gerar over rights to use the wells that his father Abraham had dug in the vicinity (26:17–22). Three times Isaac dug new

It is noteworthy that God acknowledged Abraham's obedience in reference to his keeping God's "requirements, commands, decrees and laws" (26:5). Moses characteristically used these terms to refer to the legislation which God gave at Mt. Sinai, something that happened more than four hundred years after the death of Abraham (cp. 15:13). How could Abraham keep God's laws before they were given?

The answer is that Abraham's faith allowed him to obey God in all his ways, thereby keeping the law in his heart. In much the same way Moses commanded all Israel to love God "with all your heart and with all your soul" (Deut. 30:6). (From John Sailhamer, "Genesis," in *Expositor's Bible Commentary*, Zondervan, 1990, pp. 186–187.)

wells before he found an undisputed location. Each well was given a name: first Esek ("contention"), then Sitnah ("enmity"), and finally Rehoboth ("wide open places").

This progressive resolution led Isaac and his men back to Beer-sheba, the place where Abraham had made a covenant of peace with Abimelech following a similar dispute over water rights (26:23–25; cp. 21:25–34). At Beer-sheba Isaac's men dug a fourth well (named Shibah, "oath" or "seven," 26:33), and Isaac renewed the covenant with Abimelech (26:28–31).

- *Contention between Isaac and Abimelech*
- *was resolved peacefully; as a result, the*
- *blessing of God flowed between Isaac and his*
- *neighbors.*

The Separation of Isaac's Sons (27:1–28:9)

In Gen. 27 the story of Isaac again turns to the exploits of Jacob and Esau. This time Jacob's tricks forced him to flee for his life, away from his family and out of the land of promise.

The Stolen Blessing (27:1–46)

When Isaac grew old and became blind, he sought to bestow the patriarchal blessing on his eldest son, Esau (27:1–4). Esau was out preparing the necessary meal that was to accompany the blessing. Jacob, pretending to be Esau, came to Isaac (27:5–26). Isaac promptly blessed Jacob rather than his brother (27:27–29).

When Esau returned, he was livid but could receive from his father only a secondary blessing, bestowing on him a life of hardship and toil (27:30–40). Esau resolved to kill Jacob as soon

The Philistines lived along the coastal plain of southern Canaan (generally from Joppa to Gaza), a region called Philistia. The word *Palestine* comes from the name Philistia. Gerar, a city southeast of Gaza, was in the vicinity of Philistia. Historical evidence attests to the Philistines living in this area during the early years of Israelite settlement in Canaan. Except for the references in Gen. 21 and 26, there is no evidence placing the Philistines there during the time of the patriarchs.

A father's blessing often served to transfer goods and authority to his sons before his death. Such blessings also invoked God's favor upon the one being blessed. Isaac's blessing performed this latter function since the legal transfer of goods and authority had already been covered by the "sale" of the birthright (25:29–34). Words spoken in a formal setting were considered to have a force in and of themselves and once spoken, could not be revoked.

as Isaac died, but Rebekah told Jacob to flee to her brother Laban in Haran (27:41–45).

Jacob and Esau acted true to their characters, with the result that their family was broken and their parents were left in dismay. God chose to honor the blessing and the birthright for reasons that only He could fully understand. Together these formal instruments of bestowal secured Jacob's right to be the trustee of the covenant promises. Jacob did not deserve God's favor. For the rest of his life, God worked to bring Jacob to a point where he would at least appreciate what he had gotten and what he had done to others to get it.

- Jacob seized Isaac's blessing from Esau
- through trickery. While Jacob's actions were
- questionable, God used them to accomplish
- His will.

The Flight of Jacob (28:1–9)

Jacob, having seized everything, left it all behind and fled for his life to Haran, his mother's ancestral home. Before Jacob left, Isaac blessed him again, this time asking God to bestow on Jacob the same blessing He had given Abraham (28:3–4).

Esau, now out of the promised line, married two women—a local Hittite woman (26:34–35) and one of the daughters of Ishmael (28:9). Isaac, on the other hand, instructed Jacob to go to Haran and marry one of the daughters of Laban, Rebekah's brother (28:2). Jacob left on his journey, intent to marry within the line of promise. But unlike his father, he left the land of promise behind to do it (cp. 24:2–8; 29:1).

- *Jacob received the blessing and with it the*
- *potential for great gain, but it was secured at*
- *great cost. Jacob's attempt at self-preserva-*
- *tion left him, for the moment, alone in the*
- *world.*

QUESTIONS TO GUIDE YOUR STUDY

1. What was Isaac's role in the story of Genesis?
2. Characterize the family relationship of Isaac, Rebekah, Jacob, and Esau. In what ways was their family typical of families today?
3. What does the struggle between Jacob and Esau teach about the sovereignty of God?

THE LIFE OF JACOB: THE STRUGGLE FOR GOD'S PROMISES (28:10–36:43)

Jacob's early years were spent in conflict with his twin brother Esau. Through premeditated trickery, Jacob wrestled both the birthright and the favored blessing from Esau and fled home as a result. On his own for the first time in his life, Jacob was followed step-by-step by God, who blessed him in spite of his cheating ways. Jacob eventually became reconciled to his brother, to his God, and to himself.

Living a Life of Promise in a Hostile World, Part IV (28:10–31:55)

Like Isaac and Abraham before him, Jacob faced challenges in a hostile world outside the land of promise. Jacob's trials, however, came at the hands of his own extended family. Having tricked his brother, Jacob himself was tricked by his uncle.

Jacob's behavior provided an important lesson for the Israelites of Moses' day. Moses portrayed Jacob in all of his struggles to gain God's blessing. The first readers of Genesis, Jacob's descendants, had received God's laws on Mt. Sinai, only to fail to keep them again and again. Just as God had patiently developed Jacob into a man of faith, so He would do whatever was necessary to bring Israel to Himself.

Jacob's Ladder (28:10–22)

Jacob journeyed to Haran to find a wife. On the way he stopped at Bethel, the same place where Abraham had built an altar upon first entering Canaan (12:8). At this spot, Jacob dreamed of a ladder that reached from earth to heaven with God standing at the top (28:11–13). God spoke to Jacob, reaffirming the promises he had made to Abraham and Isaac and adding a new one: "I am with you and will watch over you wherever you go" (28:13–15).

Upon awaking, Jacob made a vow that if God kept His promises, then he would serve the LORD and offer tithes to Him (28:18–22).

How are we to assess Jacob's response to God? Jacob's initial reaction was one of reverence ("How awesome is this place!" 28:17), but did his vow show genuine faith? True to his character, Jacob offered to serve God only if God first helped him (28:20–22).

- At Bethel, God bestowed on Jacob the same
- promises he had schemed so hard on his own
- to secure. Now Jacob had to grow in his faith.

Jacob and Laban (29:1–31:55)

When Jacob arrived in Haran to look for a wife, he stopped at a well, as Abraham's servant had done years before (29:1–3; cp. 24:10–14). Here he met Rachel, the daughter of Laban, his mother's brother (29:4–12). Jacob stayed in Laban's home and agreed to work for him for seven years in exchange for Rachel becoming his wife (29:13–20).

At the appointed time Jacob was married, but the next morning he discovered that he had been given Leah, Rachel's older and less attractive sister, instead (29:21–25; the name Rachel means "ewe lamb" while Leah means "wild cow").

Laban again offered Rachel to Jacob but only if he would work another seven years. Because of his love for her, Jacob readily agreed (29:26–30).

Jacob the trickster had finally met his match in Laban. Just as Jacob had taken advantage of Isaac's poor eyesight to seize the patriarchal blessing, (27:1, 18–24), so his own eyes were blinded to the difference between Rachel and Leah on his wedding night. Jacob eventually got what he wanted, but he also got the lesson he needed.

Ancient Near Eastern wedding ceremonies usually consisted of a lengthy celebratory meal with much drink and gaiety, followed by the act of consummation late that night. The bride dressed in beautiful clothes, including a veil (Ps. 45:13–14). Evidently during their consummation, either Leah insisted that she not remove her veil or Jacob was not in total control of his own faculties, or both.

Jacob's visit to Haran to find a wife ended up lasting twenty years (cp. 31:38). While in Haran, Jacob fathered eleven sons. Leah bore Jacob six sons and one daughter: Reuben, Simeon, Levi, Judah, Issachar, Zebulun, and Dinah (29:31–35; 30:14–21). Rachel, who was barren, allowed Jacob to bear two sons through her maid Bilhah: Dan and Naphtali (30:1–8). Jacob then had two sons by Leah's maid Zilpah: Gad and Asher (30:9–13).

Finally, "God remembered Rachel and opened her womb" so that she bore a son whom she named Joseph (30:21–24). From these eleven sons plus Benjamin—who would be born to Rachel after Jacob returned to Canaan (35:16–20)—the twelve tribes of Israel descended.

Numerous legal texts from across the ancient Near East attest to the practice of a barren woman allowing her husband to have children through one of her maids. These surrogate children would be considered the children of the barren woman. Sometimes the texts indicate the formal legal adoption of such children by the childless wife.

The birth of Jacob's sons was a contest in competing wills. The rivalry between Jacob's wives—one sister who was loved and another who was rejected—was as intense as the rivalry between Jacob and his spurned brother Esau. Leah and Rachel each struggled for supremacy just as Jacob and Esau had done. God waited, and finally had His way. Jacob slowly learned that God was in control.

Jacob increased his own flocks of sheep and goats through selective breeding at the expense of Laban (30:25–42; 31:8–12). The concluding assessment of Jacob's work for Laban (30:43) mirrored God's blessing on Abraham (12:16) and Isaac (26:14). It suggested that in spite of Jacob's efforts, it was God who provided his wealth of sons and flocks.

Jacob, fearing Laban's reprisal for increasing his wealth at his father-in-law's expense, fled Haran for Canaan with his family and wealth (31:17–21). Laban pursued and caught up with Jacob in Gilead, across the Jordan River from Canaan (31:22–30). After a passionate plea insisting on his own integrity in the face of Laban's deceitfulness, Jacob made a covenant of peace with his father-in-law (31:36–55). Both deceivers had met their match in each other.

Both Jacob and Laban acknowledged that it was God who had directed the events in their lives (31:24, 29, 42, 51–54). They parted in peace, each returning to his own home.

■ *While in Haran, Jacob acquired great*
■ *wealth, a large family, and a new apprecia-*
■ *tion of the work of God in his life. Having*
■ *met his match in Laban, he was now ready to*
■ *meet Esau—and God—face-to-face.*

Jacob's Return to the Land of Promise (32:1–35:29)

Jacob had made peace with Laban, but he was still at war with himself, with Esau, and with God. Before returning home, all the events of Jacob's life came to a dramatic finale in a nighttime meeting with God; he left a changed man. Jacob became reconciled with his brother Esau, but the actions of his sons in their new home proved that each generation must respond to God on their own.

Wrestling with a "man" (32:1–32)

While approaching Canaan, Jacob was informed that Esau was coming to meet him with four hundred men (32:3–6). Fearing the worst, Jacob took evasive plans by dividing his company into two groups (32:7–8). Jacob then prayed, admitting his helplessness to God and asking for deliverance from Esau (32:9–12). Jacob offered a generous gift to appease Esau (32:13–21), sent his family on ahead, and spent the night alone in the bottom of the rugged Jabbok River valley (32:22–23).

At this desolate location, Jacob wrestled all night—with someone or something he could not identify. Genesis 32:24 calls Jacob's opponent a "man." According to Hos. 12:4, the "man" was really an angel. Perhaps Jacob thought he had been jumped by Esau, who was intent on revenge.

At just the right moment, the "man" defeated Jacob with a simple touch (32:25), and Jacob recognized that he had been beaten by a divine opponent. The "man" then changed Jacob's name from Jacob to Israel, from "deceiver" to "one who strives *with* God," and blessed him (32:26–29).

Jacob wanted to know his opponent's name, but he had his own name changed instead. In the ancient world, a personal name was more than a label; it was an identification. When someone was given a name, he was granted a destiny expressed by that name. For a person to know someone else's name and call on it was to tap into that person's destiny. By wanting to know his opponent's name, Jacob was trying to gain a measure of control over him and to retain control over himself.

The "man" left unnamed. He embodied all of Jacob's opponents: Esau, God, and Jacob himself. Jacob's own strength was proven to be puny, and he knew that he had survived the night—and a lifetime of struggle—only because of the grace of God (32:30).

■ *After a lifetime of struggle, Jacob finally sur-*
■ *rendered to God. He became a changed*
■ *man—converted, we would say—and a wor-*
■ *thy custodian of God's covenant promises.*

Reconciliation with Esau (33:1–20)

Jacob continued toward Esau, still unsure of the outcome. Esau's response was wholly unexpected. He ran to meet Jacob, embraced and kissed him, and wept for joy at the safe return of his brother (33:4). Their conversation revealed that both men had changed; both recognized that God had blessed the other (33:5–15).

At the same time, both Jacob and Esau realized that their futures lay along different paths. Esau returned to Seir, the land of Edom lying southeast of Canaan (33:16).

Jacob went to Shechem, the city in the middle of Canaan where Abraham had first stopped on his journey from Haran years before (33:18; cp. 12:6). There Jacob bought a plot of land and pitched his tent.

The struggle between the brothers ended in peace; the struggle between their descendants—the Israelites and the Edomites—was yet to begin (cp. Deut. 23:7; Obad. 1–21).

Søren Kierkegaard said, "It is no use remembering a past that cannot become a present." Later Old Testament writers were painfully aware of how the struggles of Jacob the man were replayed by Israel the nation. Hosea 12 is an excellent example. Hosea wove key events from the life of Jacob into a description of the behavior of the Northern Kingdom, Israel, during the eighth century B.C. By doing so, Hosea tried to call the Israelites back to God.

- *Jacob and Esau finally became reconciled,*
- *but they went their separate ways. Jacob*
- *returned to the land of promise and put down*
- *roots there.*

The Sons of Jacob in Shechem (34:1–31)

Back home, Jacob was ready to pass the torch to a new generation. Isaac had experienced trouble controlling two sons. Jacob now had twelve sons, and each carried a bit of their father's temperament.

When Shechem (the man), son of the king of Shechem (the city) raped Jacob's daughter Dinah, her brothers responded as Jacob once might have: "deceitfully" (34:13). Shechem wanted to marry Dinah but was told that he and all the men of the city must first be circumcised (34:8–17). Shechem readily agreed. While the men were still sore and unable to get around because of their circumcision, two of Jacob's sons, Simeon and Levi, killed them and plundered their goods (34:18–29).

Jacob responded in dismay (34:30; cp. 34:5), for he now knew what it took to live peaceably among people who were not under God's covenant. Simeon and Levi remained unrepentant (34:31).

This story carries an underlying theme in Genesis: persons in the promised line were not to marry Canaanites or other foreigners (24:3; 27:46; 28:1). Shechem wanted the men of his city and the sons of Jacob to become "one people" (34:16). In spite of the violent manner in which the story was resolved, God saw to it that His chosen line remained pure.

Archaeological and literary evidence shows Shechem was a sizeable and influential city-state during the time of the patriarchs. The city was strongly fortified and had a "temple-tower." The kings of Shechem were known for their attempts to control the entire central hill country of Canaan.

■ *The actions of Simeon and Levi in destroying*
■ *the men of Shechem spelled trouble for the*
■ *future of Israel. But their actions also antici-*
■ *pated the conquest of Canaan under Joshua.*
■ *God's purposes for the world are carried out*
■ *in spite of the actions of His chosen people.*

The Promise Restated (35:1–29)

Genesis 35 brings Jacob back to Bethel, the first stopping place on his journey to Haran over twenty years before. Jacob's own story is almost over, and within a few chapters he and his sons will immigrate to Egypt. Genesis 35 anticipates Israel's return to Canaan under Joshua.

Jacob saw to it that everyone in his household gave up their foreign gods (35:2–4). In the same way, Joshua in later years would command the Israelites to "choose for yourselves this day whom you will serve. . . . But as for me and my household, we will serve the LORD" (Josh 24:15). As Jacob journeyed to Bethel, the cities in the region were overcome with fear (35:5), just as the Canaanites would respond with fear to the march of Joshua (Josh. 5:1; 10:1–2).

At Bethel, God restated His covenant promises to Jacob (Israel), guaranteeing that Jacob would be given the same land promised to Abraham and Isaac (35:9–15). Under Joshua the twelve tribes of Israel, descendants of the twelve sons of Jacob, received that land.

Genesis 35 ends with important genealogical notes. Jacob's last son, Benjamin, was born as Jacob's family journeyed south from Bethel (35:16–21). Rachel, Jacob's beloved wife, died in childbirth and was buried in Bethlehem.

Jacob arrived back in Hebron to be reunited with his father, Isaac, who then died (35:27–29).

■ *By returning to Bethel, Jacob's journey out of*
■ *the land of promise was finally over. He had*
■ *left Bethel a deceiver, possessing nothing but*
■ *God's promises (28:10–22); now he returned*
■ *greatly blessed and a partner with God.*

The Descendants of Esau (36:1–43)

Genesis 36 lists the descendants of Esau. More than two hundred names are given. Early in his life Esau had given up his birthright and received only a secondary blessing from his father, Isaac (27:39–40). Nevertheless, from Esau eventually came a mighty nation, the Edomites.

Unlike Jacob, Esau married Canaanite women (36:2–3). He then moved to Seir, an arid plateau southeast of the land of promise (36:6–8). This land, modern southwestern Jordan, became the homeland of the Edomites.

The list of the descendants of Esau is divided into several sections, each of which is a type of genealogy. Included are lists naming the immediate descendants of Esau (36:9–14), the chiefs of the sons of Esau (36:15–19), the sons of Seir the Horite who lived in the land of Edom (36:20–30), the kings who reigned in Edom before Israel became a nation (36:31–39), and a second list of the chiefs of Esau (36:40–43). These lists testify to the importance of Esau and Edom in biblical history.

Rachel was buried in Bethlehem, a town where two personalities intimately connected to God's promises were born—David (1 Sam. 16) and Jesus (Luke 2).

In spite of Moses' plea to Israel to "not abhor an Edomite, for he is your brother" (Deut. 23:7), conflict between Israel and Edom was common in Old Testament history (cp. Num. 20:14–21; 24:18; 2 Sam. 8:13–14; 2 Kings 8:20; Pss. 60:9–12; 137:7; Obad. 1–21). It was Edom that helped Nebuchadnezzar, king of Babylon, defeat Judah. Then Edomites moved into the land of Judah after the Judeans were exiled (Ps. 137:7). In the years just before the New Testament era, the Edomites became known as the Idumeans; one of their prominent men, Antipater, had a son who became known as Herod the Great.

■ *Moses took great care to preserve the names*
■ *of the descendants of Esau. Israel's neighbors*
■ *were not faceless enemies but real people*
■ *with real names. It was to such people that*
■ *Israel was called to carry God's blessing.*

QUESTIONS TO GUIDE YOUR STUDY

1. Explain how Jacob met his match at the Jabbok River.

2. How was Jacob's second visit to Bethel different from his first visit?

3. If Esau stood outside the line of promise, why is so much information given about him in Genesis?

The Hebrew word used to describe Joseph's coat (37:3) is translated in various ways: "a coat of many colors" (KJV), "a long robe with sleeves" (NRSV), and "a richly ornamented robe" (NIV). In 2 Sam. 13:18 the same word is used to describe the customary clothing of a princess. Egyptian pictures of Canaanite clothing show garments with bright colors and long sleeves. While the exact meaning of the Hebrew word is uncertain, the function of Joseph's garment is sure: it was intended to set him apart from his brothers by showing his favored status.

THE LIFE OF JOSEPH: OBEDIENCE AND DELIVERANCE (37:1–50:26)

The Book of Genesis ends with the story of Joseph, the fourth and last patriarch. In a sense, the story of Joseph continues the family feud that began with Isaac and Ishmael. In each generation of patriarchs, family members were pitted against one another in struggles over the right to receive God's blessing and carry His promise. God acted behind the scenes throughout Joseph's life to deliver His people from famine and knit them together into a mighty nation (Gen 50:20).

Conflict among the Sons of Israel (37:1–38:30)

The Joseph narrative begins with two stories of conflict between Jacob's sons. The protagonist in each story, Joseph, then Judah, eventually would become the channel for a special blessing from God.

Joseph Sold into Slavery (37:1–36)

Joseph, the firstborn of Rachel—Jacob's beloved wife—was his favorite son. Jacob's blatant show of favoritism caused his other sons to become jealous (37:4). Their resentment grew deeper when Joseph dreamed his brothers would bow down to him one day (37:5–11).

Joseph carried a message of goodwill to his brothers, who were pasturing their flocks in a fertile valley surrounding Dothan, north of Shechem. They threw him into a pit with the intention of killing him later (37:12–24). At the suggestion of Judah, Joseph was sold to a passing caravan of Ishmaelite traders, who carried him to Egypt (37:25–28).

Upon returning home, the brothers showed Joseph's coat, which they had torn and bloodied, to their father (37:31–32). Jacob was convinced that Joseph was dead (37:33–35); in fact, as a slave in Egypt (37:36), he was as good as dead.

■ *Joseph was sold into slavery, but his dream had*
■ *indicated that he would rule over his brothers.*
■ *Joseph could only wait—and trust in God.*

Judah and Tamar: A Lesson in Righteousness (38:1–30)

Genesis 38, a break in the Joseph story, offers a lesson in righteousness. Judah's oldest son, Er, died, leaving a wife named Tamar (38:1–10). According to the principle of levirate marriage, she should have been married to Er's younger brother Shelah, but Judah refused (38:12–14). Tamar put on the garb of a prostitute and was impregnated by Judah, whose own wife had also died (38:15–23).

Early in his life Joseph faced a crisis of faith. His dream of prominence and success was taken away, and he faced a bleak future. His father Jacob was also crushed. Tricked by his own sons (cp. 27:18–26), he wanted to die (37:34–35). In the meantime, where was God? His actions were unseen, like they often are, but effective and sure nonetheless.

The custom of levirate marriage allowed a man to inherit his dead brother's property and manage it for his widow. In this way, the family property would remain intact. As part of the arrangement, the man would marry his brother's widow, and any male children they would have would be counted as the sons of her dead husband. This custom was practiced in ancient Israel and became part of the legislation of Deuteronomy (25:5–10).

When Tamar was found to be pregnant by harlotry, Judah commanded that she be burned to death. With great drama, Tamar revealed that Judah was the father of her child (38:24–25). Tamar's life was spared, and Judah acknowledged that she was more righteous than him. By not allowing her to marry Shelah, he had caused the problem to happen.

The act of prostitution is not an issue in this story. The focus is on concern for descendants. Judah was insensitive to the needs of Tamar and Er's unborn family. He recognized that his actions undercut God's promise that Jacob's family would become a great nation. As the head of his own family, Judah had certain obligations to ensure the well-being of all. In failing to meet these obligations, Judah recognized his own unrighteousness. Eventually, however, it was from the line of Judah that both David and Jesus came.

- *It took a lifetime for Jacob to become a*
- *changed man. Jacob's sons, now custodians*
- *of the promise, inherited his ways. To whom*
- *much is given, much is required.*

Living a Life of Promise in a Hostile World, Part V (39:1–50:26)

The rest of the Book of Genesis follows the life of Joseph in Egypt. Unlike Abraham, Isaac, and Jacob, Joseph's actions among people who lived outside the land of promise were exemplary.

Joseph in Prison in Egypt (39:1–41:45)

God caused Joseph to be so successful in Egypt that Potiphar, the captain of Pharaoh's guard, placed him in charge of his household (39:1–6).

Egyptian documents reveal that many foreigners ("Asiatics") served as slaves in Egypt during the time of the patriarchs. Some of these reached positions of high authority within Egyptian households.

Joseph was thrown into prison on false charges when he refused to commit adultery with Potiphar's wife (39:7–20). God responded by blessing Joseph in prison, and the chief warden put him in charge of all the prisoners (39:21–23).

God gave Joseph the ability to interpret dreams. While in prison, Joseph explained the meaning of dreams experienced by Pharaoh's chief butler and chief baker. In both instances the dreams, which revealed the future, came true just as Joseph had said (40:1–23).

Upon hearing of Joseph's abilities, Pharaoh called on him to interpret a troubling dream he had experienced (41:1–24). Joseph revealed that Egypt was to undergo a severe famine. He advised Pharaoh to store sufficient grain in the meantime to ensure his people's survival (41:25–36). Pharaoh reacted by elevating Joseph to a position over the entire land of Egypt, second only to himself (41:37–45).

The story of Joseph offers a glimpse into ancient Egyptian government and administration. The titles of officials and the description of their duties given in Gen. 39–41 are consistent with what is known from Egyptian sources. Joseph's position under Pharaoh seems to have been that of royal vizier, or executive administrative officer.

■ *Joseph, both slave and prisoner, responded*
■ *not in bitterness but by being the best servant*
■ *he could be. Because he was faithful, he was*
■ *rewarded by God and men.*

Joseph as Ruler in Egypt (41:46–45:28)
As a high administrative official in Egypt, Joseph was used by God to provide for Egypt and for his own family. When Joseph's brothers came to Egypt, they bowed down to him, just as Joseph's dream in Canaan had indicated they would do.

Written records from across the ancient Near East speak of the ideal king as one who provided justice for those who were poor, needy, and helpless. For the psalmist, this ideal king was God: "Blessed is he whose help is the God of Jacob. . . . He upholds the cause of the oppressed and gives food to the hungry (Ps. 146:5–7).

JOSEPH'S PROVISION FOR EGYPT (41:46–57)

Joseph used his position of authority to store up huge quantities of grain in preparation for the coming famine (41:46–49). When the famine struck, Joseph was able to provide ample grain for the Egyptians and for all the surrounding countries which purchased food from Egypt (41:53–57).

During this time Joseph married and had two sons, Manasseh and Ephraim. Their names expressed the joy Joseph felt at receiving God's blessing while he lived in Egypt (41:50–52).

■ *God blessed Joseph in Egypt with sons and*
■ *wisdom to care for those who were under his*
■ *charge.*

JOSEPH'S PROVISION FOR HIS FAMILY (42:1–45:28)

Because of the severity of the famine in Canaan, Jacob sent his ten oldest sons to Egypt to buy grain (42:1–5). They bowed before Joseph; while they did not recognize him, he knew them (42:6–8). Joseph supplied his brothers with grain at no charge but insisted that they return to Egypt with Benjamin, his only full brother and the joy of Jacob's old age (42:6–28).

Although he was dismayed by the possibility of losing another favorite son, Jacob allowed Benjamin to return to Egypt with his brothers (42:29–43:15). Joseph treated them royally, especially Benjamin (43:16–34).

In order to test his brothers' integrity, Joseph arranged to have Benjamin falsely accused of stealing the royal silver cup (44:1–13). Judah, the brother who had years before first suggested that Joseph be sold into slavery (cp. 37:26–27), volunteered to be punished in Benjamin's place lest their father experience even greater grief (44:14–34). Centuries later Judah's descendant, Jesus, would give his life so others could live.

Once Joseph was assured that Judah was willing to give his life for his father's favorite son, he revealed his true identity. He declared that God had orchestrated all the events of their lives in order to preserve His people from extinction (45:1–8). Joseph insisted that his entire family immigrate to Goshen, a fertile area in the eastern Nile River delta (45:9–24). Jacob, overcome with joy at the possibility of seeing Joseph again, agreed to go to Egypt (45:25–28).

Psalm 105:7–23 is a poetic account of the patriarchal history section of the Book of Genesis. Verses 16–23 cover the life of Joseph in Egypt. The psalmist wrote that Joseph was given a position of authority in Egypt "to instruct his princes as he pleased and teach his elders wisdom" (Ps. 105:22). By responding to his brothers with generosity and a forgiving spirit, Joseph showed the Egyptians what a life lived under the blessing of the LORD God could be like.

■ *The injustices that Jacob and Joseph experi-*
■ *enced at the hands of their brothers turned*
■ *out to be events planned and controlled by*
■ *God. Although His hand was unseen, God*
■ *worked through Joseph to bring His blessing*
■ *to the nations.*

Jacob's Sojourn in Egypt (46:1–50:26)

Genesis ends with Jacob and his family immigrating to Egypt and settling in the land of Goshen. Jacob blessed his sons and looked forward to the day when his descendants, back in the land of promise, would see the fulfillment of all God's promises.

THE IMMIGRATION OF ISRAEL TO EGYPT (46:1–47:31)

Once before, Jacob had faced a long and uncertain journey out of the land of promise. Then, when he stopped at Bethel on his way to Haran,

God appeared in a dream and spoke to Jacob the promises which He had first given to Abraham (28:10–17; cp. 12:1–3).

Now God spoke to Jacob in a dream again, promising that his descendants would become a great nation in Egypt (46:2–4). Both times God promised to be with Jacob and bring him back to his own land (28:15; 46:4), although this time only his dead body would return (47:29–31; 50:1–14).

This assurance was crucial for Jacob, but also for the first readers of Genesis—persons who were seeking to enter Canaan for the first time after the Israelite's four-hundred-year sojourn in Egypt (cp. 15:13–16).

This sojourn was about to begin. Jacob went to Egypt, taking his entire family with him (46:5–7). A total of seventy persons made their homes in Egypt (46:8–27). This is the same number of persons who appear in the table of nations (Gen. 10), the list of people groups inhabiting the world after the Flood. As the descendants of Noah constituted all of humanity, so the descendants of Jacob formed a new humanity—the children of Israel, God's chosen people (cp. Exod. 19:5–6).

Jacob and his family settled in a fertile region of the Egyptian delta called the land of Goshen (47:11). Some of Jacob's family were employed by Pharaoh to care for royal cattle which fed there (47:6). Joseph provided for Jacob's household out of the bountiful stores of Egypt (47:12).

Jacob blessed Pharaoh (47:7, 10) and offered a succinct appraisal of his own life: "My years have been few and difficult" (47:9). Jacob real-

God told Moses that His people, the Israelites, would be "a kingdom of priests and a holy nation" (Exod. 19:6). Peter used the same words to describe Christians: "But you are a chosen people, a royal priesthood, a holy nation, a people belonging to God." Peter continued by tying this Christian identity to the promises which God had given to Abraham: "That you may declare the praises of him who called you out of darkness into his wonderful light" (1 Pet. 2:9). Christians, just like Abraham, are blessed so they might be a blessing to others.

ized that his lifetime of scheming had brought trouble upon himself. Although he had been forgiven by God, he had to live with the consequences of his actions.

■ *Jacob and his family immigrated to Egypt,*
■ *where his descendants would stay for four*
■ *hundred years. God blessed the Israelites in*
■ *Egypt, and they grew into a mighty nation.*

THE BLESSING OF JACOB (48:1–49:33)

Before Jacob died, he passed the blessing of God on to his sons. Jacob first blessed Ephraim and Manasseh, the sons of Joseph (48:8–20). He counted these boys as his own offspring (48:5–6), and their descendants became two of the twelve tribes of Israel. Jacob intentionally gave Ephraim, the younger son, the favored blessing just as Isaac had unintentionally given Jacob, also the younger son, his favored blessing (cp. 27:1–40).

Again, the one who did not deserve the blessing received it—evidence that God's blessing issues not from human status but from grace.

Jacob then blessed each of his twelve sons (49:1–27). Jacob's words recalled his sons' past deeds (either for good or evil) and spoke of their futures as individual tribes. Each blessing was aptly suited for the character of each son. Judah, the fourth son of Leah, and Joseph, the first son of Rachel, received the most favorable blessings (49:8–12, 22–26). Of these two, however, Judah was to be preeminent.

Jacob's blessing of Judah is messianic. Jacob foretold that the tribe of Judah would hold the rulership over Israel "until he comes to whom it

The word *Shiloh* which appears in some English translations of Gen. 49:10 is an untranslated Hebrew word which means "until he comes to whom it belongs."

At the end of his life Moses also blessed the twelve tribes of Israel (Deut. 33:1–29). Moses' blessing was reminiscent of that of Jacob, speaking directly to the future life of each tribe in the land of Canaan.

belongs" (49:10). King David and all of his descendants who reigned in Jerusalem were from the tribe of Judah. From this royal line came Jesus, the coming ruler spoken of by Jacob. Jesus received all authority over Israel and "the obedience of the nations" (49:10).

- *Jacob's blessing anticipated the mighty*
- *nation that would descend from him. Jacob*
- *also spoke of the coming One who would be*
- *heir to all of God's promises.*

THE DEATHS OF JACOB AND JOSEPH (50:1–26)

Jacob at last died (49:33) and was embalmed by the Egyptians (50:1–3). Joseph headed a great funeral procession which bore Jacob's body back to Canaan, where it was buried in the cave of Machpelah beside Abraham and Isaac (50:7–14).

Joseph's brothers feared that with Jacob dead, Joseph would treat them harshly for selling him into slavery years before. They came to Joseph and begged his forgiveness (50:15–18). Joseph responded, "You intended to harm me, but God intended it for good to accomplish what is now being done, the saving of many lives" (50:20).

With this reply, Joseph summarized God's activity throughout the Book of Genesis. God the Creator is sovereign. His purposes to bless mankind through the chosen line of Abraham—the line of promise—are accomplished in spite of the actions of His people.

Joseph also eventually died (50:26). His last words were spoken to encourage the Israelites by reminding them that someday they would return to the land promised to Abraham, Isaac, and Jacob (50:24–25; cp. 12:1). It was the first readers of Genesis, the contemporaries of Moses, who fulfilled Joseph's prophecy.

■ With the passing of Jacob and Joseph, the ■ people of Israel became firmly settled in ■ Egypt. The stage was set for the work and ■ ministry of Moses, Israel's great deliverer.

QUESTIONS TO GUIDE YOUR STUDY

1. How did Joseph respond to adverse circumstances differently than his father?

2. How did Joseph help to fulfill God's promises to Abraham that the people of Israel would become a great nation and inherit their own land?

3. How did the story of Joseph inspire hope for the Israelites of Moses' day? How does it inspire hope for you?

❖ ❖ ❖ ❖ ❖ ❖

Just over one hundred years ago the acclaimed American writer Stephen Crane offered the following assessment of the universe:

> A man said to the universe:
> "Sir, I exist!"
> "However," replied the universe,
> "The fact has not created in me
> A sense of obligation."

(Stephen Crane, "A Man Said to the Universe," 1895)

Many of the horrors of the twentieth century can be traced to the actions of people who believed that the universe was cold, impersonal, uncaring, and pointless. The ancient Book of

Genesis shouts out exactly the opposite. God not only created the universe but placed Himself under the moral obligation to care for it. God's promise to bless the world through people of faith remains in force today. The God of the promise will carry us into the twenty-first century.

The following list is a collection of Broadman & Holman reference sources used for this work. They are provided to meet the reader's need for more specific information or for an expanded treatment of the Book of Genesis. All of these works will greatly aid in the reader's study, teaching, and presentation of Genesis.

Cate, Robert L. *An Introduction to the Old Testament and Its Study.* An introductory work presenting background information, issues related to interpretation, and summaries of each book of the Old Testament.

Dockery, David S., Kenneth A. Mathews, and Robert B. Sloan. *Foundations for Biblical Interpretation: A Complete Library of Tools and Resources.* A comprehensive introduction to matters relating to the composition and interpretation of the entire Bible. This work includes a discussion of the geographical, historical, cultural, religious, and political backgrounds of the Bible.

Farris, T. V. *Mighty to Save: A Study in Old Testament Soteriology.* A wonderful evaluation of many Old Testament passages that teach about salvation. This work makes a conscious attempt to apply Old Testament teachings to the Christian life.

Holman Bible Dictionary. An exhaustive, alphabetically arranged resource of Bible-related subjects. An excellent tool of definitions and other information on the people, places, things, and events of the Book of Genesis.

Holman Bible Handbook. A summary treatment of each book of the Bible that offers outlines, commentary on key themes and sections, illustrations, charts, maps, and full-color photos. This tool also provides an accent on broader theological teachings of the Bible.

Holman Book of Biblical Charts, Maps, and Reconstructions. This easy-to-use work provides numerous color charts on various matters related to Bible content and background, maps of important events, and drawings of objects, buildings, and cities mentioned in the Bible.

Mathews, Kenneth A. *Genesis 1–11:26* (The New American Commentary, vol. 1A). A scholarly treatment that emphasizes the text of

Genesis, its backgrounds, theological considerations, issues in interpretation, and summaries of scholarly debates on important points.

Sandy, D. Brent and Ronald L. Giese Jr. *Cracking Old Testament Codes*. A guide to interpreting the literary genres of the Old Testament. This book is designed to make scholarly discussions available to preachers and teachers.

Smith, Ralph L. *Old Testament Theology: Its History, Method, and Message*. A comprehensive treatment of various issues relating to Old Testament theology. Written for university and seminary students, ministers, and advanced lay teachers.

Stevens, Sherrill G. *Genesis* (Layman's Bible Book Commentary, vol. 1). A popular-level treatment of the Book of Genesis. This easy-to-use volume provides a relevant and practical perspective for the reader.